Homage to Thomas Eakins, Etc.

Homage to Thomas Eakins

Homage to Thomas Eakins, Etc.

BY RAPHAEL SOYER

Edited by Rebecca L. Soyer

South Brunswick

New York • Thomas Yoseloff • London

©1966 by A. S. Barnes and Company, Inc.

Library of Congress Catalogue Card Number: 65-24829

Thomas Yoseloff, Publisher
South Brunswick, N. J.

Thomas Yoseloff Ltd
18 Charing Cross Road
London W.C.2, England

The painting *Homage to Thomas Eakins* and all the studies for it reproduced herein are from the Joseph H. Hirshhorn Collection, and are reproduced by permission.

For David S. Lieber

and Joseph S. Lieber

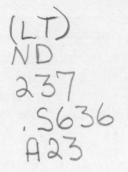

6343

Printed in the United States of America

Foreword

This is an attempt to explain why I wrote this book. All my adult life I have made painting my livelihood, working at it as a matter of routine, from morning till light fails. I've had no hobbies, but periodically, since my childhood, I have had a desire to write. It would flare up at intervals and I would be impelled to begin a diary, keep it going for months, and then destroy it. The last diary I started and destroyed in the 1940's, when I was engaged in painting a series of portraits of artists, many of whom have since passed away. (What wouldn't I give to have this diary now, with its conversations, and descriptions of Stella, Marsh, Sloan, Gorki, Weber, and Hartley!)

It seems to me that for artists writing is closely related to, or is an extension of, their work. The aphorisms of Michelangelo and Degas, the letters of Van Gogh and Pissaro, the diaries of Delacroix and Gaugin are remembered and read. They are unique and of great value, for in them the artists try to explain themselves and their art, and to make sense of the whole phenomenon of art.

When I mentioned to Van Wyck Brooks one day while he was posing for me in my studio that I was writing a journal (later published as *A Painter's Pilgrimage*), he eagerly said, "You have your manuscript here? Let me see it. I like to read what artists write."

This is, in some way, a sequel to that journal.

In these very confusing times, when the survival of the art that I have known and grown into is in doubt, when the reason for such painting in these days of new media of communication is questioned, I still cling to painting fatalistically, and I am trying to understand why. And why, at this late date, am I inspired by Fantin-Latour's *Homage to Delacroix*? And why venture upon a group portrait, an *Homage to Thomas Eakins*?

This book is about two years in my life, in which I travelled, immersed myself in the works of the masters, came in contact with other artists, and worked in my studio. Necessarily, some insights will be found which may throw light upon these questions, without, of course, offering any conclusive answers.

Contents

Illustrations

Homage to Thomas Eakins, Etc.

Paris

June 1963

THEY ARE CLEANING PARIS THESE DAYS, WASHING OFF THE DUST OF CENTURIES from the old buildings. They are doing it carefully and delicately, trying to preserve the stone with which the public buildings and churches were constructed. They are not sand-blasting, but washing them gently, with the same care with which they have been cleaning their treasured paintings. Every few years I find some newly washed old masters, cleaned with great sensitivity, not scrubbed or polished like the paintings in the museums of Washington or London.

Paris Museums have a great fascination for me because there is such a variety of art, unlike the Italian museums where art is predominantly Italian, or Belgian museums where it is predominantly Flemish, or Dutch museums where, of course, their native art predominates. The Louvre is ten museums in one. It contains the greatest collection of French art, from the Avignon Pieta to the wealth of Corots, including Poussin, LeNain, de La Tour, David, Ingres, Delacroix, Gericault, Courbet, and in such profusion. Besides the French works, there are the unique masterpieces: the da Vinci *Madonna of the Rocks,* Van Eyck's *Madonna of Chancellor Rolin,* Rubens' *Kermess,* Rembrandt's *Bathsheba,* Tintoretto's self-portrait as an old man, Bellini's *Risen Christ,* and the gigantic, serene, great technical achievement of Veronese's *Marriage at Cana.*

The distribution of paintings among the three national museums in Paris is a very intelligent one: in the Louvre are all old masters and schools through the period of Corot; in the Jeu de Paume, the Impressionists; and in the Musée d'Art Moderne, the Post-Impressionists through the contemporary artists. The Louvre contains artists of many nationalities, the two other museums are strictly for French artists—not a Mondrian, Paul Klee, or Kandinsky, no Beckmanns, no Munchs, no Kokoschkas, Corinths are to be seen in them. A few foreign-born painters, however, who lived and worked mainly in Paris, have been acepted—Chagall, Soutine, Pascin, Modigliani. I am accustomed to, and prefer, the international character of the Museum of Modern Art in New York, where artists of other countries, besides the Americans, are found.

13

Prado

Juan de Flandes

Geertgen tot
Sint Jans

Louvre

RAPHAEL SOYER

Page from sketchbook.

Homage to Eakins

June 1963

IN THE JEU DE PAUME I LOOKED AGAIN AT THE GROUP COMPOSITIONS BY FANTIN-Latour, and wondered about my *Homage to Eakins* for which I have made a few tentative studies. Already I'm running into some difficulties because of lack of knowledge of how to do a big painting like that. Where should such a big canvas be placed in relation to the subject if I want to work on the figures from life after the composition has been formed? Were these paintings of Fantin-Latour really done from life? They seem to have been.

Another thing that interests me is the feeling of unity and intimacy prevailing in these compositions, *Homage à Delacroix, Le Coin de Table,* and the Batignolles painting. Was this achieved by the chiaroscuro in them? The artists depicted here seem to have known one another. Manet is surrounded by his friends. In *Le Coin de Table* the romantic poseurs are alike in age, dress, and beard, except for the very young Rimbaud. The group in *Homage à Delacroix* consists not only of those who remembered him but also of his youthful admirers—Manet watched Delacroix's shadow through the lighted window of his studio, and observed his movements.

I can see from the preliminary studies that the painting I am planning will have no such feeling of intimacy or unity. The light will be flat and sharp. There is also a difference of age, from the youthful Dobbs to the eighty-year-old Hopper. I wonder if even the painting, the *Gross Clinic,* which I shall paint in the background, will create some feeling of unity. None of these artists who have posed for me for this painting has been so involved with Eakins as those in the Fantin-Latour painting were with Delacroix. They were his young contemporaries and they intensely admired the older Delacroix. None of these whom I am painting had any similar relationship with Eakins; he had no such influence on them. This forgotten-during-his-lifetime Philadelphia painter is now looming as the great figure in American Art.

These are the thoughts that came to my mind as I looked at the Fantin-Latour paintings in the Jeu de Paume. Of course, the fact remains that I haven't even begun

15

the large canvas. What inspired me to attempt this project was *Homage à Delacroix* and the Eakins exhibition in Philadelphia, which I went to see twice. I felt it would be good to make a painting honoring this great American realist. Also, for many years I've had a gnawing desire to do a large group portrait.

I contacted a few artists and Lloyd Goodrich, the biographer of Thomas Eakins. I wrote first to Edward Hopper, saying, "I'm writing to you first because I cannot conceive this composition without you in it. In other words, I consider this projected painting not plausible unless I have you in it."

I promised to use as little of their time as possible, to make a quick oil sketch of each artist, and then to compose the large canvas with Eakin's *Gross Clinic* in the background. All the artists agreed to pose, but since each one was involved with his own work, it was difficult, as I had thought it would be, to fit their schedules with mine.

Each one, it seemed to me, responded characteristically: Hopper, for instance, warned me that there might be some artists who would want to be included not for their love of Eakins, but for reasons of publicity. Baskin wanted to know who else would be in the picture. Jack Levine and Goodrich both called and said, "Of course I'll pose for you," and so did John Koch. The active interest of Lloyd Goodrich was most encouraging and helpful. It was he who suggested the inclusion of an old portrait I had done of Reginald Marsh.

The first one to come was Hopper. I had arranged with Abe Lerner (a lover of art, a collector, and by profession a book designer) to fetch him and take him back home. I quote from the fragmentary diary I kept during these sittings.

Leonard Baskin

Jack Levine

Edward Hopper

Henry Varnum Poor

Moses Soyer

Edwin Dickinson

Edward Hopper

January-February 1963

HOPPER HAS JUST LEFT AFTER TWO HOURS POSING FOR A STUDY OF THE PRO-
jected painting, *Homage to Eakins*. The sitting was quite an ordeal for me. I painted
carefully and intensely, almost without resting. He has, to use Jack Levine's descrip-
tion, a "granitic" head. Curved and bent though his body is, his height comes through.
I imagined him in the role of those fantastic saints who flagellate themselves, or medi-
tate in deserts, in the paintings of Carpaccio and de La Tour. There is a loneliness
about him, an habitual moroseness, a sadness to the point of anger. His voice breaks
the silence loudly and sepulchrally. He posed still, with folded hands on the table. A
few times he raised his folded hands to scratch his ear with the tip of one of his inter-
twined fingers. We hardly conversed. He was interested in the paints I used, their make,
and expressed the opinion that lead white is preferable to zinc because the latter has a
tendency to peel. His paintings, he said, withstood time rather well on the whole.
He hasn't gotten to paint yet this year and was troubled about it "like hell." My wife
came up and invited him to come down for tea. He resolutely refused. I asked him
when he would come again. "I'll call you," he said. I was disappointed, for I hoped
he would say "next Saturday."

Feb. 1. Hopper didn't call. Every day I waited in vain. Rebecca, my wife,
strongly advised me to telephone him, for "he may have forgotten about his promise
to call, and it may even be that he expects Lerner to come for him tomorrow." But
I didn't want to intrude upon him, and I phoned Lerner not to call for Hopper the
next day.

Feb. 2. Upon coming home in the late afternoon, Rebecca told me that Hopper
called and said, "Where was Lerner? I waited for him all morning." I called Hopper
back immediately telling him how I waited all week for his call in vain, that I didn't
want to intrude upon him, and how sorry I now felt that I had not followed my
wife's advice not to stand on any ceremonies and to call him to remind him about
coming to pose.

17

Detail from a life study of Edward Hopper.

"You're not intruding upon me," came Hopper's answer. "I'll come next Saturday."

Feb. 9. Again uneasy embarrassment. At 9:45 (Hopper and Lerner were to be here at 10), Lerner phoned that the cold weather temporarily disabled his car, and he couldn't start it, and so he couldn't call for Hopper, but that he would be glad to drive him home, for in a few hours he thought the car would start up. I immediately rang up Hopper. "Eddie, it's for you," I heard Mrs. Hopper at the other end. Worriedly I explained the situation to Hopper.

"I'll get a taxi and will come down." I went down to wait for him, and soon saw the taxi from which the long Hopper extricated himself with some difficulty. We were soon in the studio again. I worked with combined frenzy and timidity. This time there was more conversation in which Lerner joined when he arrived.

"You don't have to bother to come for me," said Hopper.

"I do it for myself," answered Lerner. "It is my pleasure."

Again Hopper was interested to know whether I use zinc or lead white in the ingredients of the paints. He regretted that there are no brushes to be had today of the quality of the pre-war Rubens brushes. He was interested in my easel.

"Where did you get this easel? I made mine myself. It is so big it has to be taken apart to move it out of the room."

The conversation turned to Eakins, and photography. "I would think Eakins used photography to some extent in his paintings, but Goodrich says 'No, he did not' . . . . I don't know."

Ever so often Hopper ends a statement complainingly with "I don't know."

"His (Eakins') paintings are so dark, it is a disadvantage." He wondered how an Eakins' exhibition, a comprehensive one, would be received in Europe. He repeated a few times that Forbes Watson wrote (to him?) that when Eakins' *Concert* was shown somewhere in Italy, the spectators did not know what to make of it, and laughed.

"They simply laughed at it," he said in worried tones a few times.

I said I vaguely understood this reaction to Eakins' *Singing Woman*, that static, almost mannequin-like portrait with the open mouth that looked as if it would never close. "How alive," I said, "compared to her, are the *chanteuses* of Degas, so mobile in facial expression and gesture."

In talking about Kuniyoshi's work, Hopper said: "His work is oriental, and oriental painting does not go so far as western art. It stops."

I agreed with him and said: "Yes, that's very true. It does not go so far as a work by Van Eyck."

And Abe Lerner, in his well-constructed-sentence-way, said that "Western art has an element lacking in oriental art, which once you become accustomed to, you cannot do without, and that is psychological penetration . . . in addition to the aesthetic elements."

"Of course," said Hopper, "it's a very formalized art. Hiroshige is more realistic, because I think he was influenced by Western art."

We talked about photography again, about its use for painting. I said that photography could be helpful at times. "Your jacket, for instance, does not retain the same folds each time you come to pose."

"I took a photo of a landscape once and could not use it," Hopper said. "Photography is so light, no weight to it."

I then mentioned the early photographs of the Parisian, Atget, and the American, Brady, whose portraits and Civil War pictures do have a three-dimensional quality. Lerner praised Nadar and Bresson, but Hopper ponderingly insisted, "They can't get the same weight as painters can . . . I don't know."

"As Hopper can," I thought. His paintings of dunes, bridges, houses, have this weight.

Hopper often talks about movies. "Jo and I go to movies a lot." He mentioned the *Long Absence* and *The Twelve Angry Men*. "Did you see the French movie, *Mon Oncle*?" he asked. "It's a good satire on modern technology."

After two and a half hours of painting without a stop, I asked Hopper if he was tired.

"No," he said. "I can pose more. You don't have to hurry."

But just at that moment my wife came up, carrying our grandson, snub-nosed, lively-eyed, full of promise and potential, but as yet unable to walk or talk. "May I introduce David to you?" she said. "This is David. David, say hello to Mr. Hopper."

"He doesn't have to say it, if he doesn't want to," said the octogenarian in a sepulchral voice; and there was some warmth and humor in his eyes, I thought, as he glanced from under his forehead at the infant.

Feb. 16. Abe Lerner came in with Hopper at 10 A.M. As always, we immediately went to work. Hopper looked older, quite haggard, his lips purple, almost bluish, and at times he seemed to have difficulty focusing his eyes. Conversation was desultory. I told him that I heard that the Kastor Fund recently purchased a painting of his for the Metropolitan Museum.

"Yes," Hopper said, "a painting of a lighthouse. The Museum acquired it from my dealer, who, in turn, got it from its former owner. I painted it long ago—about forty years ago."

He said he met a niece of Edward Munch, the Norwegian painter, a trained nurse, who took care of him when he was ill in the hospital. He happened to talk about her because when he came he was holding an opened letter, which may have been from her. "We became friendly," he said, "and correspond. She gave me a book on Norwegian art. It is terrible. They haven't ever produced good painters. Draftsmen, maybe."

A professor, head of an art department, recently asked him to participate in an art symposium with the non-representationalist Motherwell and others. "I said *nix*. Painting has become a matter of words to such a great extent," he said sadly. His thoughts wandered. "Do you know the French comic, Tati?" he asked. "His picture, *My Uncle,* is in color, not bright, good color. It is a good parody on modern life."

I told him that since I've decided to paint this *Homage to Eakins,* I have been looking at paintings of portrait groups, the Franz Hals paintings, the *Syndics* by Rembrandt, etc. There is the problem of combining the various faces and figures, different in size and complexion. "Jack Levine is quite tall," I said, "but would appear small next to you."

"Yes," Hopper answered, "he has a narrow face," and with sudden interest he asked: "Have you started him?"

"I was looking at Rembrandt's *Syndics,*" I continued. "He did a marvellous job of harmonizing the different sized and complexioned people."

"Where is that painting . . . in Amsterdam?" Hopper asked.

"Yes," I replied, "and it's delicately cleaned. In France and Holland they do not scrub the old paintings, as they do in New York."

We then talked about writers on art and critics. We discussed their virtues and shortcomings.

"They don't seem to write what they think," Hopper said. "Of course, there are pressures. They weave a fabric of words that doesn't seem to have much to do with painting. I don't know," he continued, after some brooding, "they don't actually paint themselves, they are looking inside from the outside, you know."

"Did you know McBride?" I asked. "He wasn't bad."

"He was amusing . . . Guy Pène du Bois was better." (He mentioned du Bois' name several times with something like fondness.) "He knew more about painting, for he was a good painter himself. I was a fellow student of his at the Chase School. We both studied with Henri, too, who was a good teacher, talked a lot about life in connection with art, and revolution in art. But he was a limited painter, just the model and the background."

"I think that all of them," I said, "lacked quality, style—Henri, Bellows, Sloan."

"Their movement was important in American art, but they were not great painters at all. Du Bois had no use for Bellows; Glackens became arty after a while."

Hopper was last in Europe in 1910. He lived in Spain, Paris, Holland, Belgium, and for some time in Germany and England.

"I would like to see Italy. I've never been there," and he added, as if to himself, "Gulack doesn't like Italy." (Gulack is an artist who recently became friendly with the Hoppers.)

We talked about Italian art. "It is too lush, and sweet at times," I said. I mentioned Van der Goes' *Adoration of the Shepherds* at the Uffizzi, which surpasses its contemporary Italian paintings of similar content. "I love Masaccio, he is so human," I said.

"Mantegna is very masculine and vigorous," said Hopper, "and Piero della Francesca seems to be the idol today."

We discussed the state of preservation of these paintings and murals. Hopper described a Dutch or Flemish painting he had seen at a dealer's. "I don't know the artist's name. It was just of a square, a beautiful sunlit pavement and houses—no figures."

He talked about Mexico where he painted some watercolors. Had he met any of the Mexican painters who were quite popular here at that time?

"No. At a hotel where we stayed once, Siqueros stayed, too. I didn't meet him."

"Did you know any of the French painters when you lived in Paris?"

"No, I didn't know anyone. Gertrude Stein was on the throne when I was there."

It was twelve-thirty, and I told Hopper that I had finished for the time being. I asked him if I might call upon him again should I need him.

"Yes, you may," he answered.

I was flattered and even moved that this seemingly unfriendly and aloof old man posed for me so willingly and patiently. One artist once told me that when he asked Hopper to sit for a drawing, "his face assumed the expression of one who stepped on a rattlesnake." When I asked Hopper if he had ever done a self-portrait, he said: "Only once, and, according to Jo, so mean looking that I never showed it."

I think by now Hopper wants to resemble the popular image of him: an objective, aloof man, cold, without an emotional interest in life or the art of today. His work is like himself—frugal, lonely, weighty, truthful, unadorned, unsentimental. I remember seeing him recently at a gathering sitting on a hard bench all by himself in a roomful of chattering cocktail-drinking men and women. There was an aura of aloneness about him. How much like his paintings he seemed!

He's "worried like hell," he complained the other day, because he hadn't begun to paint this year, but I believe that he paints mentally all the time. The composition, the content, has to be clear and accurate in his mind before he begins to lay it out on the raw, white canvas. On the Cape, he sits against the wall of his white house, perched on a hill facing other hills, and studies the landscape weeks on end. He waits patiently for the fall "when the shadows grow longer and landscape becomes more interesting; in fact, wonderful."

Leonard Baskin

April 1963

WHEN LLOYD GOODRICH STRONGLY URGED ME TO INCLUDE LEONARD BASKIN IN the Eakins painting, I did not realize to what extent Baskin had become involved with Eakins. From what I had seen of Baskin's work until that time, I could not find any influence of Eakins in it, and I still am not able to see any relation of Eakins to Baskin's work. He seems to be attracted to him personally rather than artistically. Baskin's predilection for little-known, not widely popular, and non-glamorous figures in art may have led him to Eakins, who worked in loneliness and was known to few in his lifetime.

His preoccupation with Eakins is revealed in a series of etchings which Baskin made of him, imaginary portraits of different periods in his life, showing movingly his industry, integrity, persistence in his strivings in the face of rejection. To Baskin, Eakins represents a tragic figure. He showed me a photostat of a photograph of Eakins in his late years, and said, "Look at his eyes!" And his eyes were big, wide-open, and seemed to me at that moment, terribly sad.

One evening, in his house, Baskin showed me his treasures: several paintings by Eakins; old photographs of him, and photostats of photographs; a letter in Eakins' handwriting, carefully enclosed in transparent plastic; Eakins' tiny brushes, one of which seemed to me encrusted with paint; and a small wooden penholder whittled by Eakins himself, with a nib in it, black with dried ink. All these objects he handled with reverence and tenderness.

The first time I met the Baskins, Leonard and Esther, was at a party, and they were sitting by themselves, a young, handsome and shy couple. Ten years later in the summer of 1962, we visited them, my wife and I, at their summer home on Deer Isle in Maine. I did not recognize him. He looked like a hermit, with reddish-brown hair and beard, stooped and hollow-chested, with an indoor pallor and red-rimmed light eyes.

It was a gray and moody day. He took us for a walk from one end of his land

Detail from a life study of Leonard Baskin.

to the other, along the water's edge. From the house to the water he had built a trellised walk, and had already planted climbing roses along its path, which would eventually cover the entire overhead structure. I visualized this rose arbor in bloom, and it seemed to me like injecting a bit of Fragonard into a Ruisdael landscape. "I'm building this for Esther. She will be able to use this as a sort of promenade in her wheelchair from the house to the water," Baskin said.

Inside the house where Esther had already been seated at the table, we had tea, and we talked. Esther showed us her recently published book, *Creatures of the Night,* illustrated by Leonard, and mentioned another book she was planning to do.

I went to Northampton to make the study of Baskin for the Eakins painting, and I was a guest at his home several times. We took a walk the first evening through a small woods surrounding his house, and soon his small son joined us, taking his father's hand. After a while I felt his other hand in mine as he walked between us taking part in the conversation.

His house was filled with many books, paintings, and drawings. Everything there revealed his particular interests—the drawings were by old masters not generally known; many of the books were in old print, decorated with woodcuts, and he had them for that reason rather than for their content. The walls were literally covered by shelves with books, by drawings and paintings. Some pictures had no room to hang, and were standing along the walls and on tables. The furniture was antique and unusual. After dinner he brought out portfolios with more drawings by obscure masters, anatomical drawings, and etchings.

Baskin posed well, and made me feel absolutely at ease. He was interested in the way I worked from a living model, for he himself never works from life. He told me he never sculpted a female figure. We talked about art and artists and I found he has strong opinions, definite likes and dislikes, and is intolerant of pretense. We often used Yiddish and Hebrew expressions. He prefers Yiddish because, he said, it is a folk language.

I worked two days, mornings and afternoons, with time out for lunch. While painting him, I was always aware of his paleness in spite of his living in the country all year around. Once while walking with him through the campus, I noticed he deliberately avoided the sun. He showed me his bronze sculpture, set up against a brick wall on the campus, of an untidy owl whose talons and beak were powerful, shiny, and polished, in contrast to the ruffled texture of the rest of him.

On my way home I thought a great deal about Baskin. Now that I have met him in personal surroundings his art has acquired more meaning for me. I watched him work for a while on one of his wood carvings of a male neo-mythological figure, without a model or a drawing to guide him. He worked with great assurance, as if from a vision. Personally, I am intrigued by and amazed at artists who work completely from imagination. For I, in my work, have held back from surrendering to it, or to invention, and have always based my work upon factual reality.

Baskin's art is as complex as he is, as his life is. Among other traits in it, I have been aware of what I would call a strain of Jewish lacrimosity, deep-rooted. His drawings of metamorphic faces, with eyes shedding tears that form lakes, recall to my mind such an intrinsically Jewish phrase as *Teichen-Treren*—rivers of tears. He makes use of in his art whatever life brings to him, and thus creates a sort of personal mythology tinged, of course, with many influences from ancient arts, the sculptures and mummies from Egypt, the lavafied forms of humans and animals from Pompeii, and other similar influences, symptomatic of an almost medieval concern with death. Like Bosch, Holbein, Baldung-Grien, Grunewald, with their dances and triumphs of Death. Throughout the ages artists have been thus involved with mortality—now recently Lovis Corinth in his paralyzed old age; also James Ensor and Edward Munch, of course, painted pictures with death as the central figure. It may be that Baskin belongs to this group.

The Delacroix Exhibitions

June 1963

THIS WAS A DELACROIX SUMMER—ONE HUNDRED YEARS SINCE HIS DEATH IN 1863. Paris was busy with Delacroix exhibitions of his paintings, his murals, his drawings and graphics. The Louvre had the greatest display. It is hard to imagine what other artist's work could have covered so much wall space. Half of the tremendous Gallery Appolon was given over to the show.

What was interesting to me were the drawings: hundreds and hundreds of them, studies for the large paintings, and small studies in oil, were hanging alongside the finished compositions. Near *Liberty Leading the People* were many studies of the heroic figure of the woman, holding the flag aloft. Near the *Death of Sardonopolus* were magnificent studies of nudes for the painting in black-and-white and in pastel. There were many drawings of animals in all sorts of action, done in pencil, pen-and-ink, and in water color for the paintings of hunting scenes; there were also bright and delicate sketches in water color of oriental men and women, and of interiors for the Algerian paintings—drawings for the *Ship-Wreck of Don Juan,* for *Medea Killing Her Children,* and many others, including studies for the wonderful *Massacre at Scio*.

This gave me insight into the way Delacroix worked: how this visionary romantic conceived the large paintings; how he enlarged upon his visions from small sketches to more elaborate ones for the final composition; how he painted separate detailed studies for the figures in the composition. It is interesting to compare him with Courbet, who painted the *Burial at Ornans* and the *Studio* directly, without any preparatory studies.

My favorite Delacroix paintings still are his early ones: the *Visit of Dante to Virgil, Liberty Leading the People,* and the *Massacre at Scio.* To me they are his three faultless, spirited works. There is a complete fusion in them of conception and execution. He labored long and arduously on them without losing the fiery spontaneity of the original conception. In his other paintings there are outstanding, unforgettable

27

details such as the raped women in *The Crusaders Entering Constantinople,* or the nude in the *Death of Sardanopolus,* but the other parts of these paintings do not carry forth the quality of these details, thus lessening the unity, the wholeness of the entire picture.

There is a startling picture, or rather a huge fragment of one of a lion hunt, a bloody chaos of struggling animals and men, of fiercely clawing lions, of men desperately trying to spear them, of a fallen horse (always horses with dilated nostrils, with wide-open frightened eyes). It is painted riotously, with the kind of fury such subject matter demands, with colors of crimson lake that bring to mind the occasional violence of a Soutine. There is a sadistic element here inherent in romantic paintings of this kind.

As part of the centennial celebration, the house in which Delacroix lived and worked was converted into a museum containing his memorabilia and was open to the public. We visited this with our friend, the painter Joseph Floch, who excitedly told us about some Delacroix frescoes decorating the libraries in both the Senate Building and the Chamber of Deputies.

An amusing sidelight on the character of the French was revealed in our efforts (successful) to see these murals. Neither of these buildings was open to the public at the time we got there, but Floch, in his determined way, was able to convince the guards that it was important for us to be admitted that day. Not only were we allowed in, but we were given a guide to lead us to the murals, to light them for us, and to conduct us politely out. How different was this attitude from what prevailed in New York, where a guard would point at a sign and rudely say, "What's the matter with you? See the sign? Can't you read? It's closed!"

Milan

July 1963

THE BIG EXPERIENCE IN MILAN WAS TO SEE AGAIN LEONARDO DA VINCI'S *Last Supper*. Before entering the Chapel of Santa Maria della Grazie we wondered how we would react to this painting. Was our reaction to it two years ago conditioned by the universal adoration of da Vinci, by the accustomed awe in which we held him?

When we looked at the *Last Supper* this time, in the morning light of the empty chapel, it seemed to us even more satisfying than we had remembered it. We wondered if its present condition, with so much of the final layers of color rubbed off and faded by time, does not add to its abstract beauty. We had seen two well-preserved contemporary copies, one in the Louvre and the other in the Ambrosiana in Milan. Both were rather dull and academic. But here we were deeply moved by the gray softness of the Apostles' robes, with tinges of orange, old rose, green, yellow—all, now, tentative colors; by the deeper warm grays of the walls and ceiling; the marvelous perspective congenital to the composition; the wonderful space and light behind Christ; and contrasting with the serenity generated by all these qualities, the feeling of utter agitation in the painting expressed by the faces, the movements, and gestures of the disciples. The feet of all the figures have become completely obliterated. There is nothing but different shades of grayness left; the hands and faces, though distinct and living, have lost their absolute delineation, have become somewhat blurred, thus acquiring a metamorphic quality, lending to the whole work an atmosphere found in some of our own contemporary art.

The rest of the art in Milan was rather dismal. Of course, in the sea of seicento paintings in the dark and gloomy Brera are the magnificent *Madonna and Saints* by Piero della Francesca; Mantegna's foreshortened Christ; moving compositions by Bellini, and a very fine portrait of a red-bearded man by Lorenzo Lotto.

Shockingly neglected are the outside walls of the Ambrosiana Museum, their age-old mustard yellow peeling and showing dirty gray plaster. The interior, evidently a former well-kept palace with marble columns and tiled marble floors, resembles a

29

huge antique shop with its indiscriminate collection of paintings, sculpture, fragments of sculpture, and even dishes, bric-a-brac, and furniture. But it does have the huge, original cartoon of Raphael's *School of Athens,* a portrait of an unknown lady by de Predis, and a *Musician* by da Vinci.

Renato Guttuso

July 1963

I HAD ALWAYS WANTED TO MEET RENATO GUTTUSO, WHOSE WORK I HAVE KNOWN for some time, but somehow on our previous trips to Europe we were unable to make contact. This time, however, we did get to see him at his summer home in Velate-Varese, a small town in the hills not far from Milan, where everyone seemed to know Guttuso, and we were soon directed to his house. We were greeted by both Renato and his wife with unaffected warmth. We spent three hours with them in interesting conversation. We saw his work in his studio, and we stayed for lunch.

He thanked me for sending him my book, *A Painter's Pilgrimage,* but even before he got it, he said that John Rewald, the art historian, had sent him an Italian translation of the allusions to him in it. That surprised and pleased me very much. One of the passages referred to the negative attitude other Italians had toward Guttuso and toward one another. He seemed to accept it for a fact. But I said again what I had written in the book: that in Italy today a very few artists have so far outstripped their contemporaries in achievement and fame, that there is a sense of resentment on the part of those who are left behind.

I spoke very freely and frankly. I said that when I mentioned his name, or that of Manzu, to some people in Italy, there were such comments as "Oh, Guttuso, he's a Communist!" or "Manzu? Why, he's a Catholic!" To which I would reply that my interest was purely in their art, and that, moreover, Catholicism has certainly created a great art, and surely good painting should not be incompatible with Communism.

All this, and other conversations, were held in Italian, French, and English. Guttuso understands quite a bit of English and is able to interject an English phrase effectively into the general thought, and Madame Guttuso, with her excellent command of English, translated for him. Whenever necessary, Guttuso tried to communicate in French with my wife, who translated into English for me.

I told him that one day while working in my studio, I heard his name mentioned in a broadcast on culture in Europe. It turned out to be a discussion on Guttuso in

31

RAPHAEL
SOYER

1963

RENATO GUTTUSO
VELATE Varese

Renato Guttuso.

which his work was described rather intelligently, linking it to Delacroix and Gericault. To this he commented that he had gone to Paris just to see the Delacroix exhibit, and while he was greatly impressed by its vitality and spirited romanticism, he feels, at this particular moment, a greater affinity to Gericault, and especially to Courbet. I was delighted by his mention of the great realist who painted the *Burial at Ornans*.

Then I said, "You know, I often think of you as a present-day Tintoretto. In your drawings and paintings there is a tumultuousness and restlessness which can be described as 'Furioso de Guttuso,' to paraphrase an old Tintoretto epithet." To which Guttuso shrugged his shoulders and quietly said he was greatly honored, but embarrassed by this comparison.

He asked me about my work. I told him with some hesitation that I was of an older generation than he, and of a different course of development; that I began to paint comparatively late; that it was only after World War II that I became aware of other artists besides the French Impressionists. For it was then, after the War, that the Museum of Modern Art in New York put on the great exhibitions of Kokoschka, Munch, and others. I told him that I was quite accepted in America as an artist in the thirties, but there came a period of decline for some time due, perhaps, to the ascendance of the various *isms* in art and, perhaps, also to a temporary slackness in my work. "At this moment, however, I have a feeling that my reputation is rising again."

I told Guttuso that we expected to be in Leningrad and Moscow, and I wanted very much to hear about his experiences there—how his exhibition was received, what he thinks of the art there, etc. He said he was officially invited to exhibit and was received very well everywhere. The authorities went out of their way to be friendly; he was honored, and was made a member of the Academy. But, nevertheless, he felt an antagonism towards his work on the part of the Academicians, and also (he said, smilingly) on the part of the young rebels who are trying to embrace abstraction. But, he said, there was a good core of those who accepted his work with approval, who were also members of the Communist party.

We talked about art in the Soviet Union. He did not absolutely decry it, as has been the fashion all this time. He found much ability there, but he thought their art criticism was old fashioned, not developed. They are still looking for content mainly, at the expense of form and aesthetics.

"Their paintings," I said, "have a literary quality which is more suited to writing rather than painting."

With a thoughtful expression on his face, Guttuso said he is now working on a pamphlet, "Art and Socialism in a Socialist State." It will be ready in October.

We continued our talk about Italian art, and he spoke thoughtfully and honestly about his contemporaries. I was amused to hear him describe a certain artist as lacking in *samo-critica*—the Russian phrase for self-criticism.

He showed us his paintings: a magnificent reclining nude, her thighs and knees expressively raised forward; two canvases painted rapidly and thinly of heads and busts of young girls; a tall canvas of a standing worker, in vivid reds and blues with an almost black background; another upright canvas, which he calls *A Deadly Wind Blows,* has its title from a poem by the Italian poet Saba (this name was mentioned to me two years ago by Carlo Levi with feeling and tenderness) and represents a semi-kneeling back view of a man (an Algerian or a Negro; Guttuso said, "It could be any man") caught in the web of the evil menace of the world as symbolized by a roughly painted black swastika in the murky, threatening background of the canvas. He likes to paint and draw very free variations of some of his favorite pictures: a self-portrait of Van Gogh, the *Death of Marat* by David, the *Head of an Executed Man* by Gericault, a detail from the large *Studio* of Courbet and his model. These are done very freely, convulsively, almost in a sleight-of-hand manner which distorts them and gives them his mark.

At lunch I constantly kept my eyes on a huge early canvas, hanging in the dining room—a modern, stormy version of the Crucifixion with a naked, lamenting Magdalene, nude soldiers on horseback, and an extraneous still life at the bottom of the canvas, beautifully painted, colorful, vivid, and plastic. It was painted in 1940 and condemned both by the fascist government and by the Catholic Church. Mme. Guttuso good humoredly told me that the Church conducted a trial against her husband for painting this Crucifixion, but the verdict was that although he painted it with the help of the devil, his intentions were good, and therefore he was acquitted.

After lunch I did a quick drawing of Guttuso. We parted very warmly, and he presented us with a huge tome of fascimile reproductions of his black-and-white and colored drawings, inscribing the book affectionatly to us. Now, as I look through this book of drawings, and also a book of his drawings and paintings compiled by Diulio Morosini, I continue to feel impressed by the vigor, the temperament, and by the contemporariness of Guttuso's art, so intensly preoccupied with people, life, and events, by his draftmanship, lightning-quick and bold; the vivid, almost brutally direct color.

Rome

July 1963

Raphael Sanzio

RAPHAEL'S MONUMENTAL PORTRAIT OF POPE LEO AND THE ATTENDING CARDINALS at the Uffizi, his other portraits in Florence, as well as his murals in Rome, have raised him greatly in my estimation. Until now I had the feeling, commonly shared, that his painting was too suave, too polished in technique, its surface almost oleographic. But there is nothing soft, prettified, or saccharine in his portraits of women.

There is a noble earthiness about his *Donna Gravida,* with her hand placidly resting on her pregnant belly; and the magnificently attired *Fornarina;* and the *Madonna of the Chair,* her full shoulders and bosom wrapped in a green shawl. Their serious, almost austere faces have no highlights, no lustre, no superficial liveliness. I began to understand why many artists, the great Ingres among them, were so moved and influenced by Raphael.

The *School of Athens* at the Vatican Museum was simply a feast to the eyes (to use a threadbare expression). It is in a beautiful state of preservation, the color is unusually fresh when compared to other frescoes of that period. The harmony and the rhythm of the composition, the noble figures of the philosophers, scientists, artists, poets, are wonderfully posed and drawn. The architectural background functions so well in relation to them. Even the way the painted plaster has cracked in that mural serves to add to its textural quality. A warmly intriguing note in the painting is provided by his own self-portrait, together with that of his master Perugino, on the right side of the mural.

And talking about self-portraits, we saw for the first time the one of Raphael in the Uffizi Gallery— the most lovable, delicately-drawn-and-painted self-portrait ever done.

35

St. Nicodemus (self-portrait of Michelangelo).

Self-portrait and Portrait of Old Man, by Filippino Lippi.

A Saint, by Donatello. (Baptistry, Florence)

Sculpture in Bargello, Florence.

Judith Shahn — Alan Dugan

One day in Rome, walking through a crowded street, I heard someone call me by my name. A small, dilapidated car stopped and we saw Judith Shahn and her poet-husband, Alan Dugan. They invited us to visit them at the American Academy in Rome. There we saw Ben Shahn and his wife, Bernarda Bryson, together with the young Italian artist, Bruno Caruso. Judy showed her work. Her father's influence seems to be on the wane, and her own individuality is becoming more assertive.

I watched the silent and cadaverous Dugan, who was helping his wife pull out her canvases. In New York I had read his slim volume of poems, and I was interested in seeing him at close range. He seemed a difficult man to know. I made a drawing of him. He posed for quite a while, and then, without warning, got up and said, "I can't pose any more," and, without looking at the drawing, walked off.

Bruno Caruso

The next day we visited Bruno Caruso, a very able artist, but whose facility may spell danger for his future work. The influences I noticed particularly in his paintings were George Grosz and Ben Shahn and, hanging on the wall among others in his collection, were examples of these two artists. Caruso's work doesn't have, as far as I could see, the simplicity or the genuineness of either one of them. He seems to elaborate too much upon the more obvious characteristics of these two painters. This may be natural for one who is under the spell of those who inspire him, and with time he may grow out of this imitation and become himself.

Corradó Cagli

Known European artists seem to live better than artists in America, more "graciously," more artistically, in seemingly more relaxed and spacious surroundings. For example, in Paris, Zadkine lives in the heart of the city, in Montparnasse, but his house and studio are set in a charming walled-in private garden; Carlo Levi's house in back of the busy Piazza del Popolo in Rome, seems to be situated in the midst of a willow grove, which has to be reached by walking through a wooded road. Also in Rome, the narrow Via Margutta where many artists work and live, hides behind its old facades many exotic studios overlooking charming gardens. In New York, this would be out of the question.

When we visited the studio of our old friend Corrado Cagli, tastefully appointed, but less impressive than the others mentioned above, he invited us to his "new apartment" a few blocks off, where we gasped at the luxurious suite of rooms, lavishly furnished, decorated with some of his recent very beautiful tapestries. Here he has

Judith Shahn and Alan Dugan.

Bruno Caruso.

installed his interesting and comprehensive collection of drawings, which range from the work of some famous old Italians, to his contemporaries, and students. Among them, in this good company, I was gratified to find my sketch of Eugene Berman, which I had presented to Cagli two years before. Corrado showed off this place with modest pleasure.

He talked about his work, the tapestries he had made, two of which are based on his abstract paintings, the color inspired by the ancient brick ruins peculiar to Rome; another tapestry romantic and classical at the same time (if possible?), a bust of a young man picturesquely clothed and hatted, in colors of burnt umber.

On a portfolio of reproductions of his work he made a pen drawing for me, and presented my wife with a volume of Ugo Foscolo, the Italian poet, illustrated with Cagli's beautiful drawings in classic style.

We left him sitting alone on an antique upholstered couch, leaning forward, his head and neck deeper than ever in his shoulders.

Munich

July 1963

TWO YEARS AGO WHEN I VISITED THE ALTE PINAKOTHEK IN MUNICH, I WAS SOMEwhat repelled by German art, except for the serene and intense work of Holbein and Dürer. The compositions of Cranach, Pacher, Altdorfer, and others appeared to me melodramatic, at times gruesome and comical, peopled with contorted, gesticulating figures, with grimacing physiognomies. This time, however, I reacted differently to them. I was fascinated by the curious imagination of these artists, and by their mysticism.

An unusual painting is the *Battle of Alexander* by Altdorfer, where on the same canvas, one sees in a turbulent, apocalyptic sky, the sun setting and the moon rising. Thousands of mailed horsemen are battling in a landscape of mountains, lakes, seas, and forests. Suspended over all this, in the middle of the picture, is a framed tablet proclaiming Alexander's victory.

And Cranach, whose portraits I am amusedly fond of, but whose compositions and nudes I frankly dislike, impressed me this time with his expressionistic painting of a blood-streaked Christ on a cross, in a barren, hilly landscape, the white loincloth fluttering starkly in the wind against a bleakly-clouded sky. An awkwardly kneeling, heavy, blank-faced cardinal in crimson and white robes, contrasts sharply with the tortured Christ.

A unique painting of Grunewald is the large *Saints Erasmus and Maurice*. It is completely devoid of his usual exuberant, if tragic melodrama, and is permeated instead with a subdued animation. The life-size figures in apparent conversation are oddly detached from each other. In the background, between the two saints, is a wonderful old open-mouthed, toothless man.

Dürer is here in full force, with his two panels of the *Four Apostles,* and some religious compositions. Outstanding is a group of portraits, including the one of himself, full-face, symmetrical, visionary, with an intense and continued gaze that is not of this world.

44

The Holbein family is represented by several altarpieces of Hans the Elder and Sigmund Holbein. Strangely enough, there is only one very small portrait by the genius of the family, Hans the Younger. In Basel we saw some very sensitive paintings by Ambrosius, who died very young. This makes quite a painting family.

There are some fine portraits. The Germans have always excelled in portraiture. Even in recent times great portraits have been produced by Leibel, Lieberman, Corinth, Dix, Grosz, Beckmann. As a matter of fact, the Apostles of Dürer are really portraits; the magnificent figure of St. Erasmus by Grunewald is a portrait of Albrecht von Brandenburg dressed in gold-embroidered and bejewelled bishop's robes; the head of the old man in that painting is that of a known abbot; and Cranach's clumsy, kneeling cardinal is also a portrait of the much painted von Brandenburg.

There are two large panels, humorless portraits by Bernhard Strigel, one of a melancholy widower, and the other of his eight children of serious mien, with a madonna and child and angels fluttering hoveringly above them. In the background of this panel is the legend: "We beg thee, pure Mary, be a mother to us." The father's panel has an inscription begging the Lord to guard him against temptation.

Two small, very fine portraits by the intriguing painter Hans Baldung-Grien are immediate and direct, one of a richly clad young prince, and the other of a bearded man with an aquiline nose, thin lips, and heavily-lidded, rolling eyes.

Among the early Flemish paintings is one of Roger van der Weyden's masterpieces, the *Coloumba Alterpiece*. It is faultlessly composed, and everything, to the smallest detail, is perfectly rendered. But to me there is something wanting, as in all of this master's work. There's a complete lack of modulation of tone; it is flat, like a tapestry; the figures seem carved in very flat relief, engraved. Space is suggested only by diminished sizes of the more distant figures and objects. This lack of tone, this lack of recession in color, this sharpness, may account for the painting's surrealist quality. There is something formal, austere, and abstract about his work, with its cool colors and cascading folds of the garments. This formalism is accentuated by the vertical architecture of the two side panels, the interior of the Annunciation, and the courtyard of the Presentation.

The other Van der Weyden is also a flat and airless painting of St. Luke (a self-portrait, I would like to believe) gazing with reverence at the posing madonna, and making a charming drawing of her.

One reads Memling's *Seven Joys of Mary* rather than looks at it, so much story-telling is in it. I liked particularly the two tiny portraits of the donor and his son.

By Hugo van der Goes there is a small painting, probably a fragment of a larger work, of a madonna and child and an angel holding a cross. Although it is in very poor condition, the troubled undertones, characteristic of this artist's work, are evident.

There is a surrealistic composition (how often I find myself using the word "sur-

Shepherd Caressing His Shepherdess, by Rubens.

Female Satyr Nursing Her Babies, from Rubens' painting in Munich.

The Feast of Venus, by Rubens. (Vienna)

Penitent Magdalene, by Rubens. (Vienna)

From a painting by Rubens, in Florence.

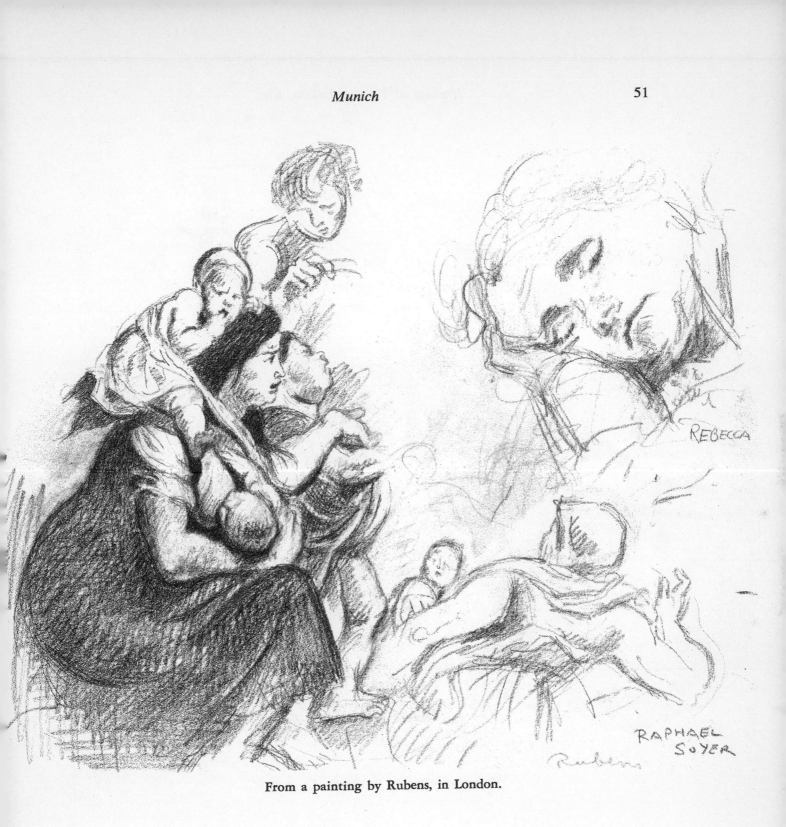

From a painting by Rubens, in London.

From a painting by Rubens, in London.

realistic" in describing Flemish paintings!) by Dirk Bouts, of a startling, slender, risen Christ, half-naked and half-covered by a red cloth, with a group of suddenly awakened soldiers, one of whom, seen from the back, is still asleep and partly covered with a gray quilt, a steel helmet on his head—altogether a strangely inanimate-looking apparition.

The sixteenth-century Flemish painters are well represented—Massys, Van Cleve, Cossaert, and others, an able but inferior and decadent group of artists. Their compostions, compared to earlier masters, are flamboyant, over-elaborate, mannered to the point of eccentricity, trivial, and sentimental.

The Rubens paintings at the Pinakothek are astonishing in quantity and quality. Seeing his work in profusion makes me think of Shakespeare, for certainly in subject matter he is as encompassing. He painted men and women in the act of love; women suckling babies; men abducting women; men hunting and at war; women crowning victors; men massacreing the innocents; women turning into clawing furies, shielding and mourning their children. He painted historical pageants, triumphant entries of victorious warriors, saints theatrically performing miracles. And the populace in these paintings—the spectators, the cheerers, the beggars swarming with children—painted with the kind of observation found in a Breughel.

His mythological subjects! The obese, carousing Silenus; the satyrs pursuing, capturing and caressing buxom nymphs; a huge female satyr crouching and nursing her horned babies, the moist nipples of her full breasts pouring milk into the gurgling throats and wetting their faces with the overflow—fantastic! And the splendid nakedness of it, the draperies accentuating bodily movements and physical fullness!

The same exuberance is in his landscapes. He painted storms, sunsets, rainbows, everything that ever happens in nature, and all that lives in the landscapes—animals, shepherds, woodcutters, milk-maids, lovers.

Often I found myself copying details from Rubens. It was like drawing from life, from living models in action.

The Pinakothek, like other European museums, has a collection of Rembrandts. *The Passion of Christ,* a series of six paintings, is here, describing the events of his life in a universally human manner. Unlike the German and Flemish paintings dealing with the same subject, they are not sermons on Christianity. They are devoid of symbolism, the only supernatural element in these dark paintings being the light which radiates from Christ and illuminates the interior.

Broadly painted predominantly in brown in a very wide range of tones are two portraits—one of the sympathetic Hendrickje Stoffels, and the other of a hairy, bearded peasant, an apostle, his rough hands folded in prayer. There is nothing monochromatic about them. They are vivid with life.

There are two of the greatest Titians, the portrait of the ashen-faced Charles V, sitting on a fringed, red satin chair, his full-length figure a black silhouette against darkish backgrounds, but, mysteriously, the silhouette has weight. Only the face is fully lighted, sometimes a hand. What always impresses me about Titian is the unostentatious way in which he paints details, like the golden thread fringe of Charles' chair, or golden sword hilts, necklaces. They don't stand out as details, they seem to be woven into the paintings. The other great Titian is *The Crowning of Christ with Thorns*. It is much superior to the early version in the Louvre. How he grew with age, like Rembrandt, Velasquez, Degas! These masters reached maturity after forty, and went on from greatness to greatness up to their deaths. How different it is with many famous artists of today, about whom one often hears the comment, "I like his early work."

Masaccio, Van Eyck, Rembrandt, Velasquez, Rubens, Vermeer, Degas—what personalities they were! The aloofness and objectivity of Degas and Velasquez; the emotional warmth of Rembrandt and the uninhibited exuberance of Rubens; the religious tranquility of Van Eyck; the enclosed quietness of Vermeer; the precocity of Masaccio—what force impelled them? One thing they all seemed to have had in common: a great response to the world about them. With the exception of Masaccio who died so very young and Van Eyck who is an artistic and historical enigma even to art historians, the work of these artists who lived long, went through organic changes in their lifetime, came to fruition at the end of their lives.

Of the three Raphaels I preferred the *Madonna Della Tempi*. It is a beautifully painted composition, with visible brush strokes, so dear to artists, of a young woman with the child nestling in her arms, walking in a landscape; wonderfully composed, the figures occupying almost the entire canvas, looming big, as if approaching you like a close-up on a screen; the colors are harmonious—pale crimson, soft blue, and yellow.

I saw again my favorite Antonella da Messina, the small *Virgin of the Annunciation*—a young woman with an inanely pious expression on her simple face, longfingered hands crossed on her chest, completely covered by a blue shawl, against a dense black background—the blue and black a telling color combination. And the *Lamentation of Christ* by Botticelli, so different in composition and spirit from all the other Lamentations with which European museums abound. It is sombre, metallic, and harsh.

On Lenbach Square I came upon a charming building in a garden, which turned out to be the Lenbach Museum, also known as the National Gallery of Art. It has the collection of paintings of Kandinsky presented to the Museum by Gabriel Munter, who was his mistress and also an artist herself. These paintings show the evolution of this typical Russian artist's work from his colorful but ordinary small landscape sketches from nature, into the now famous Kandinsky abstractions and improvisations. Together with the more extensive exhibition of his work I had seen several weeks before in the Musée d' Art Moderne in Paris, these strengthened the impression I long had of Kandinsky—a feeling of noisy emptiness. It reminds me of flimsy poetry full of loud fireworks, clever rhymes, alliteration, but shallow and without

Self-portrait done in Munich.

content. This exhibition again exposed the self-imposed limitation of non-objectivism, with its resulting sterility, for, despite all protestations, it precludes the all-encompassing art that representationalism has achieved throughout the ages. Its premise is hopeless.

Some of the more interesting items in this museum were a few late paintings by Corinth, one of a life-size nude woman and two nude children, painted with powerful desperation; a roomful of Klee; a Kokoschka, Jawlenskys, some Gabriel Munters and, to my personal delight, two early canvases by David Burliuk. History is beginning to catch up with my old friend.

In the same building is the work of Franz Lenbach, a famous name in my youth. I remember the fascination a portrait of his in the Metropolitan Museum held for me—that of an old, bearded man with glittering eyes, done in what was then known as the "Munich style," formless and muddy, the only thing projecting itself from the canvas was the head, which was searching in character. Here I saw several such portraits, one of Bismarck and some of pale, aristocratic women and neurotic-looking children.

Munich seems to be the art center of West Germany. Besides the magnificent Alte Pinakothek, there is the Neue, containing French Impressionists, German Impressionists and Expressionists, as well as work by Runge, Gaspar Friedrich, and others of the Nazarene School. In a separate wing there was *Ein Grosse Ausstellung* of contemporary Bavarian art. *"Grosse"* it certainly was, but to me quite unsatisfactory and boring. The many paintings were either weak figurative or hodge-podge non-objective, all seeming to be the efforts of a desperate compulsion to do something "different."

Berlin

August 1963

WHEN I CAME TO WEST BERLIN I WAS REALLY AMAZED BY THE UNATTRACTIVENESS of the city. I had always heard that Berlin was beautiful, and I kept saying to myself, "Is this Berlin? It is so ordinary and characterless." On Kurfurstendam there were many street cafes filled with tourists as well as Berliners who were dressed well, but dull in comparison to the promenaders in Milan, Rome, and Paris. Many displays of clothing, shoes, and other commodities were seen in store windows, but there were rather few book stores, which again surprised me, for I had always thought that Berlin was a cultural center.

The buildings were of the uninteresting contemporary "international" architecture, and I asked myself, "Could the whole of Kurfurstendam have been rebuilt since the war?" A new quasi-skyscraper, housing the Berlin Electric Company and other offices, loomed within walking distance of this famous street, which seemed to me to be a combined version of Via Veneto and Broadway. And the inevitable Hilton Hotel towered some distance away, above empty vistas of bombed-out, unreconstructed streets which were turning into jungles of weeds, bushes, and young trees, part of a remaining wall appearing here and there among them.

Over all this hovered a touching provincialism, a desire to live up to the style of big cities. There were even a few sidewalk "artists," dressed like beatniks, without shoes, unkempt, the colored dust of the pastels adding to the dirt of their unwashed faces and hands. Copying from postcards, they drew such pictures as details of the *Surrender of Breda,* and stained glass compositions. As art students they were not very well informed. To my questions about art life in West Berlin, one of them, a young girl, answered that she was just a student and did not know about that. She had never heard of George Grosz or Otto Dix. Another such "artist," somewhat older, a barefoot blond young man with Franz Joseph *backen barden,* had some knowledge of the name of George Grosz, whom he called an American artist, and

57

also had heard of Otto Dix. He complained it was difficult to sell paintings in West Berlin; in Paris, he heard, it was easier to sell.

Regretfully, I did not stay in West Berlin long enough to explore the contemporary art situation any further. The one gallery I knew of and wanted to visit was closed for the summer.

It was only when I entered East Berlin, after passing through all the red tape at Check-point Charlie, that I exclaimed to myself, "So this must be the beautiful part of Berlin!" For there it was, the well known Unter den Linden, its four rows of trees stretching out toward the Brandenburg Gate in the distance. It was Sunday morning, and except for some tourists, there were hardly any people in the streets, practically no traffic. One had an unusual sense of perspective, of streets unmarred by the ever-present automobiles.

The first door I entered was in a newly-constructed exhibition hall on the corner of Friedrich Strasse and Unter den Linden, which showed a group of international paintings and watercolors. I made a mental comparison with West Berlin. There was more life along the busy Kurfurstendam, but here there was a feeling of cultural activity in the prevailing atmosphere of unreconstruction.

I asked a policeman where the National Gallery was, and I was directed to the "Kunst Insel" (Art Island). I crossed a small elevated bridge over a canal and found myself in a wide square with beautiful churches, monuments and other structures. They had all been bombed and their state of semi-destruction seemed to add a tragic beauty to the square. The stupidity and the futile waste of war struck me forcefully. How quick was destruction, and how long it will take to bring back these buildings to their former grandeur and beauty.

The paintings and sculpture of the museums are now housed in the restored parts of these buildings. There is an excellent collection of recent German art in the National Gallery, beginning with Max Lieberman, Corinth, Schlemmer, Schrimpf; some Expressionists—Dix, Beckmann, Kirchner—as well as some current German work; also a few French paintings of the Impressionist period, including two Cézanne still lifes.

Dahlem

The great collection of Old Masters is in the nearby West Berlin suburb, Dahlem, in the Dahlem Museum. In the Pinakothek, in Munich, I was over-awed by the monumental works of Rubens, Titian, Grunewald, Dürer, large in size and in conception. In Dahlem, on the other hand, I was fascinated by the numerous, rather small but precious paintings of Van Eyck, the Master of Flemale, Petrus Christus, small portraits by Holbein, Dürer, Mantegna, Signorelli, Botticelli, Rembrandt, and Franz Hals. When I looked at Van Eyck's *Madonna in the Church,* a very small painting, I was again puzzled, as I always am, by Van Eyck: How did he manage to work in

Head of a Man, by the Master of Flemale. (Dahlem, Berlin)

all these minute details? What kind of eyes did he have? Did he use a magnifying glass, special brushes? And the all-important question: how, with all the clarity and precision of the infinite details in his canvases, was he able to maintain the wholeness and the unity of conception? Again I was struck by the state of preservation of his work. How was that achieved? His paintings even crack preciously. The blemishes are precious, such as the small discoloration on the face of *The Man with the Pink.* I hope it will not be removed.

The Madonna in the Church is not so formal as a Van der Weyden painting. It seems more realistic, more human; the interior has light and shadow, giving it depth. It actually has patches of sunlight on the floor, reflected from the doorways and vaulted windows, something that a late nineteenth-century painter would do. In *The Christ on the Cross* the two mourners, a man and a woman, have faces that show real grief, and natural gestures painted with deep, not idealized realism. Besides these two compositions, there are three inimitable, infallible portraits by Van Eyck: the bust of *Arnolfini with the Red Head-gear;* of *The Man with the Pink,* and the portrait of the *Knight of the Golden Fleece.*

There is another tragically expressive *Christ on the Cross* by one of my favorite painters, the Master of Flemale, who also has two other small paintings, very intense male portraits. Between these two portraits, and contrasting strongly with them is the delicate, sensitive in color and beautifully designed head-and-shoulders of a young girl by Petrus Christus, one of the most aesthetically satisfying pictures ever painted. Mentally I compared it to all the abstraction of Juan Gris and Braque, much to their disadvantage.

I find myself often making such comparisons, altogether out of historical perspective. For instance, when I looked at Caravaggio's painting in the Church of San Luigi Francesi in Rome, I compared it to Cézanne's *Card Players,* to the detriment of Cézanne. For after all my visits to the museums my head has become a veritable museum itself, stacked with a multitude of paintings, from all places and all times, and although it may be historically incorrect to do so, I constantly juxtapose them and compare them.

There is, however, an incomparable portrait of a young woman in a stiff white headdress by Roger Van der Weyden. It does not have the formal austerity of his compositions. It is warm, human, and soft. Other portraits are: a youngish man against a red background by Lorenzo Lotto which has the vague Lotto quality about it, both inner and external, the melancholy aspect of the face, and the odd, isolated fold in the red cloth of the background; a monochromatic head of a youth by Botticelli; a strongly characterized head of a man by Mantegna; a deep, psychological portrait of a young Jew by Rembrandt, eight by ten inches in size, but huge in execution; and another of a young, poetic, introverted Jew who posed for Rembrandt as Christ.

The other paintings by Rembrandt in this museum are so badly hung that it is

From *Manoah's Sacrifice*, by Rembrandt. (Dresden)

RAPHAEL SOYER

MANTEGNA

Madonna and Child, by Mantegna. (Dahlem, Berlin)

almost impossible to view them properly. They are all placed on a wall opposite windows, with the light shining full upon them, creating a glare so one has to maneuver in all sorts of positions in order to see them; to study them closely is very difficult. The *Man with the Golden Helmet* has a constant red glow upon it from the reflection of a red brick building opposite the museum. That destroys the spirit of the picture completely. The other Rembrandts are biblical in subject matter: *Christ Preaching to the People,* all in sepia; *Moses Breaking the Tablets, Jacob Wrestling with the Angel, Samson Threatening His Father-in-Law*—Samson is apparently a self-portrait, his face turned awkwardly as though posing before a mirror; at the same time his fist is threatening the old man whose head is sticking out of the partly shuttered window.

Italian paintings are represented here by a group of small compositions by Masaccio—harmonies in gray and black with patches of warm red; a wierdly charming Madonna tenderly supporting the head of a sleeping child wrapped in swaddling-clothes, in dull gray and yellow, by Mantegna; Ghirlandajo's *Judith and her Maid,* a small painting in which both women stride across an Italian courtyard or street, a wonderful little canvas permeated with the essence of the Renaissance. There are Botticellis and Titians, including the latter's portrait of the little girl of the Strozzi family.

There I also came across a small, dark, very early Velasquez—*The Three Musicians*—a painting I liked very much when I was young. I used to make drawings of it.

Dresden

August 1963

MY TRIP FROM WEST BERLIN TO DRESDEN AND RETURN TO WEST BERLIN VIA THE RED tape of the border was quite an odyssey. But it proved to be well worth it. Even though I had only a day and a half in Dresden, I was able to visit the great Dresden Museum twice, see an excellent exhibition of contemporary Roumanian art in the Albertinum, and find time to rest in the shade of a tree on the banks of the Elbe River.

Like in East Berlin, the Dresden Museum is also situated in the most beautiful and showy part of the city, where, as in Berlin, the historical structures and churches are still half-destroyed. The Museum is the first completely restored building. At the head of the central stairway there is a large wooden sign which in golden letters tells the public that the paintings in this Museum were saved from Nazi destruction by the Russian army which, after the war was over, returned them to the German people and to the world. Unlike the museums in Berlin, East and West, this one was extremely well attended and busy, most of the visitors coming in groups with guides and interpreters. There were many children with their teachers and, of course, individual museum-goers.

The Dresden Museum has its equivalent of *Mona Lisa* and *Venus de Milo:* Raphael's *Sistine Madonna,* biggest in size and conception, a very symmetrical, imposing composition, and Giorgione's *Reclining Venus,* one of the most perfectly composed paintings and probably the most idealized nude in western art. Here again I found a miraculous Van Eyck, a small "traveling" triptych of a Madonna, donor, and saints, still in its original frame, upon which there is hand-written: "Van Eyck me fecit"—"Van Eyck made me," and another inscription along the same frame: "Als lxh xan" ("the best I can"). One of my favorite Holbeins which I have admired in reproduction for many years is here, *Thomas Godsalve and his Son, John,* a smallish painting of an older and a younger man, against a green background, as well as the powerful portrait of Morette, a dark gray and green harmony.

Among the Italian paintings, besides the above mentioned Raphael and Giorgione, were two very interesting St. Sebastians, one a contortioned and tortured figure

64

by Cosimo Turo, and the other a placid, tall youth, expressionless though arrow-pierced, leaning against a tree, with a background of a street in deep perspective, facades of balconied buildings, and small figures of dignified people in conversation on the balconies and in the streets below—an unusual and fascinating painting by Antonella de Messina.

And here too I saw the painting of the red-tunicked long-haired youth by Pin-torucchio, delightful in color and composition, which aroused memories in me, for my mother had bought a fine and large reproduction of it decades ago, and it used to hang in our living room for many years. It became the main ornament of our home, and we were all very much attached to this picture. It is now still hanging in my niece's house.

In a roomful of Veroneses there is a particularly outstanding one of a female saint, a statuesque and vigorous woman, tenderly presenting the Suchini family to a Madonna who is surrounded by other saints. This family portrait is typical Veronese at his best, ruddy, bearded Venetians, and a full-bodied woman surrounded by her brood of children, and, as is characteristic of Veronese, wherever he has children in his paintings, there are also dogs and puppies.

The Dutch School is represented here by some of its most interesting paintings. There are two masterpieces by Vermeer: one is the unusually large (for Vermeer) and colorful *The Procuress*. The color is extraordinary, deep reds and yellow; the composition, too, is unusual, constructed with a great sense for abstraction. Looking at this painting, I was at a loss to understand why Vermeer is grouped with the Little Dutch Masters. It so completely transcends their small, anecdotal, busy pictures. The other Vermeer is *The Woman Reading at the Open Window*—with the high wall and the long drapes, painted with great freedom.

Dominating the group of Dutch painters is, of course, Rembrandt. Here I saw *Deposition from the Cross,* similar to the series of paintings in Munich; the lifesize *Manoah and His Wife,* a masterpiece of his middle period depicting two elderly people in a prayerful attitude, emotionally affected by the visit of an angel. It is nobly conceived, painted in deep reds and browns, with intense, transcending reaiism.

There is also the youthful portrait of himself with Saskia on his lap that I always had a desire to see. I compared it, with its strange air of restlessness, to the self-assured, self-contained portrait of Rubens and his wife Isabella Brandt in the Pina-kothek. The Rembrandt also is baroque in composition and character, with its air of histrionics, masquerade, and noise, but it has a certain modernism about it. It would not be impossible to imagine a Kokoschka paint a picture like that. It is tangible, but seems strangely unreal. The figure of Saskia is especially unreal and airy; her pose seems impossible, practically full-face, yet with her back to the onlooker. The color tones are soft and fused, not so deep as usual.

Of a group of paintings by Rembrandt's pupils, Ferdinand Bol, Karel Fabrizius, Van Gelder, and others, I liked Van Gelder's best—an extraordinary painting of

Presentation of Christ to the People, which I am certain was done after one of Rembrandt's etchings. It almost has the calligraphy of Rembrandt's drawing, plus a personal color sense which I had noticed before in other Van Gelder paintings such as the *Jewish Bride* in Munich, a warm, almost pinkish tone as though he saw things through rose-colored glasses.

There was a good deal of art activity in Dresden. Near the Dresden Gallery there was another museum, the Albertinum, where I saw an exhibition of Roumanian art. In the visitors' book I wrote: "It is a vigorous and vital exhibition, by any standards," and I signed my name as a "New York artist." Later I wondered why I had not written "American" instead of "New York." Can it be that I identify myself so completely with New York, where I've worked all my life? I remembered that long ago on one of my first self-portraits I signed "Raphael Soyer, a New York artist."

Vienna

August 1963

WITH THE EXCEPTION OF THE LOUVRE, THE KUNSTHISTORISCHES MUSEUM IN VIENNA contains the most varied collection of paintings I have ever seen. I shall not attempt to describe the rooms full of Veroneses, Tintorettos, Titians, and the numerous Giorgiones. What held a great fascination for me was another masterpiece by Vermeer, a strong, impeccable work, that of the artist in his studio painting from life a young woman, classically dressed, with a laurel wreath on her head, holding a huge volume in her hand. It was wonderful for me to see Vermeer actually painting from life.

In another alcove are the Rembrandts: three self-portraits (1652–55) of his vigorous years, in different moods, one with his arms akimbo, magnificently self-confident and magnificently painted; one, heavier in face, frowning and intensely living; and the last one, in shadow, his head raised, abstracted and brooding. Here is also his early portrait of his patient mother, eyes red-rimmed, gnarled hands resting on a cane; and the very poetic painting of his son reading a book.

The Kunsthistorisches Museum is noted for its room of Breughels. (I have seen books entitled *Flemish Art from Van Eyck to Breughel,* therefore he is a Flemish artist.) But he is so different from all the others. He seldom painted religious pictures *per se*. There are no portraits by him. In Munich there is a small profile of a shrewish kerchiefed woman with an open mouth as though she were talking loudly, which may be a fragment of a larger composition. He painted people, the everydayness of their life and their celebrations. His religious paintings are not devout like those of other Flemish painters who preceded him. Even though the events described in them are religious, such as the *Road to Calvary* and the *Massacre of the Innocents,* they are set in Breughel's own milieu, realistically, without any supernaturalism. In the *Massacre of the Innocents* a group of helmeted and armed soldiers invade a Flemish village on a winter day, drag the peasants and their clumsily dressed children out of their homes, and, like medieval Nazis, kill the children before the suppliant parents' eyes. In *The Road to Calvary,* we see a throng of people coming from all directions to witness an

Park in Vienna.

execution. Again Breughel depicted that event with an observant realism: the horse-drawn peasant cart that carried the two thieves to be crucified is part of the crowd, as is the Christ stumbling under the Cross—neither is dramatized. At first glance there seems to be an all-pervading confusion in this painting, but a further look shows how Breughel handled these crowds in the composition, much like a movie director manoeuvering masses of people on a set. I shuffled the many pictures that filled my mind to find a counterpart to Breughel. Perhaps Daumier with his keen observation of the life around him, comes close to him, or, in a lesser way, maybe our own John Sloan.

The Return of the Hunters is probably the most popularly known work of Breughel, with its silhouettes of the trudging men, followed by the weary dogs with curly tails sharply standing out against the snow, as is the black tree with its lacy branches outlined against the green winter sky; the view of the village; the skaters on the frozen pond; the black crows flying overhead. All this brings to mind Japanese art, which it certainly surpasses in depth. I recalled a conversation with Edward Hopper about oriental painting, in which he said, "Oriental art doesn't go as far as Western art, it stops."

How can one describe Velasquez—his technique, strong and delicate at the same time, his colors of soft rose, silvery blue, his particular kind of white and black? The five paintings of children in this museum are like no other paintings of children. There is a lightness about them, and yet a positive existence. The serious little figures are in space, with objects around them, furniture, rugs, drapes, giving them a confined, indoor quality. The delicate skill and deep perception with which these portraits are painted and composed, the unusual harmony of color, justify the awe and the wonder that artists have always had at the infallibility of Velasquez.

Through the efforts of Dr. Kurt Eissler, we were able to meet Prof. Novotney, the director of the Belvedere Museum, a well known European art historian, author of, among others, *The End of Scientific Perspective in Art,* and of a book on Cézanne. He came up, to keep our appointment, to the room where I was sketching from the *Family Portrait* by Egon Schiele. He is a charming man. We talked awhile about art in Vienna. When I expressed my surprise at not finding more art books in this city, he said, "But Vienna is not a city for painting. It is a city for music and the theatre."

I asked him whom of the Viennese artists I could visit, since I was interested in the contemporary art scene. He suggested Wotruba, as the best known Austrian sculptor. When I mentioned Paul Meissner, with whom I had an appointment later in the day, Prof. Novotney said, "Yes, you should see him. He is the president of the New Secession. He is a taschist, but you know, taschism is now passé," making a negative gesture as he said this.

We visited the studio of Fritz Wotruba, whose work can be found in various European museums, and in private collections, including the great American collection of Joseph H. Hirshhorn. He works mostly in metal, welds cylindrical forms into all kinds of figures, sometimes enlarging them into huge proportions. He showed

Fritz Wotruba.

us some of his work, earlier representational pieces, as well as the more recent work in his new style. Although he was friendly enough, we did not pursue our conversation to any great extent, for we felt he was pressed for time. However, I did make a quick sketch of him.

Paul Meissner lives in an outlying district of Vienna. His studio has a view of rolling hills and cultivated fields. He never paints it. He showed us many paintings, most of them of equal large size, on maisonite board, in varied and elaborate techniques, vague in conception. I was impressed by some of his harmonies in black, white and gray, and when I complimented him upon these colors, he said bitterly, that his color is not appreciated in Vienna, that the Viennese "have ears, but no eyes." This was, in essence, a repetition of Novotney's comment.

While showing his paintings, he talked about experiment in art, about expressing an experience or feeling, about the novelty and the limitless possibilities in this technique. I asked him about the result of all this—is it worthwhile? Can it be like a Van Eyck, of permanent value, difficult to repeat and to emulate? In reply, he pulled out one of his typical paintings, a golden-brown mass, spattered with black spots, in a background of marbleized gray and white, and said: "This is impossible to copy or repeat." My answer was, "Yes, it is difficult to repeat, for so much here is accidental and capricious."

Of course, this was not all I had in mind to say, but I could not press the point any further, being his guest, and not wanting to offend him. Again I could not understand how this artist, a seemingly sincere and talented man could have become so satisfied with this kind of involvement with just color, accidental forms, and mere evocativeness instead of content.

During this visit my mind was full of the work of Egon Schiele, which I had seen that morning at the Belvedere. That was also experimental, searching, novel—but it had content and was steeped in tradition. I recalled a conversation with a composer, a student of Schoenberg, who told me that Schoenberg once said, "Experimentation is fine. But so much can yet be said in the Key of C."

I cannot write about the art in Vienna without mentioning the memorable afternoon we spent with the Viennese-born New York psychiatrist, Dr. Kurt Eissler, who is also an art connoisseur and historian. He studied art history for two years with renowned Viennese specialists in the field, and is the author of a book, a psychoanalytic study of Leonardo da Vinci. He fairly flew through the old, familiar, narrow streets of his city, with us gasping after him, and showed us beautiful old Gothic monuments in courtyards unknown to tourists. He led us to a fine, late painting by Titian, hanging among many nondescript paintings in the almost deserted old gallery of the Academy of Fine Arts. And to change our diet from the artistic to the gastronomic, he introduced us to Demel's, a left-over spot from old Vienna, a cafe (or should I say *the* cafe? for we were told that revolutions and wars may come and go, but Demel's stays on forever), where, if one has time and patience, one

Egon Schiele in Vienna 1963 RAPHAEL SOYER

The Artist, His Wife and the Unborn Child, by Egon Schiele.

may savor the original sandwiches, pastries and ice cream for which Vienna has been famous among gourmets the world over. But we parted with Dr. Eissler in an artistic setting, in the Helden Platz, where, in a spacious area, surrounded by impressive baroque architecture, stood one of his favorite monuments, an imposing equestrian statue silhouetted against the evening sky.

Moscow

August 1963

OUR ART EXPERIENCE IN THE SOVIET UNION BEGAN WHEN WE STEPPED OFF THE plane in Moscow and were greeted, much to our unexpected pleasure, by Professor A. D. Chegodaev, the art critic and historian, author of many books, including a comprehensive history of American painting (in Russian). This was followed the next morning by a visit to our hotel room from Orest Vereisky, a graphic artist and water colorist who had come to see me in New York two years before. And again, in the afternoon, another art historian whom I had met in New York, Prof. Prokofiev, came up with a monograph of Favorsky and a guide book on Moscow and said he would like to take us to the Tretiakovskaya Gallereia, the museum of Russian art, the next day. Also, a phone call came from Chegodaev inviting us to visit with him the Pushkin Museum of Plastic Arts.

This was the pattern of our stay in Moscow. We were moved by this completely unexpected attention and hospitality, and we were involved with these people the week we spent in the capital of the U.S.S.R.

First, was the visit to the Tretiakovskaya Gallereia under the guidance of Prokofiev, where he gave us an excellent, chronological survey of Russian painting. Personally, I do not care for icons, I do not even respond to early Italian, pre-Fra Angelico paintings that resemble icons. But in the company of the enthusiastic Prokofiev, I was impressed by these sombre-sweet artifacts, some of mural proportion, taken from old churches and monasteries. Prokofiev pointed to a semi-obliterated, devout image of some saint and said modestly, as if to himself, "This is my favorite of all the icons here."

We saw the art of the 17th and 18th centuries, the work of Bobrikovsky and Kiprensky—analogous to the early American painters Copley and Stuart. In this group I liked very much the portrait of the bright, blue-eyed Pushkin by Kiprensky. We passed through rooms and rooms of genre painters. Outstanding among them were Fedotov and Venetzianov, particularly the latter, who seems to me comparable to

74

Prokofieff's
favorite
icon
in
moscow

RAPHAEL
SOYER

Icon in Tretiakovskaya Gallery. (Moscow)

Louis LeNain in the choice and treatment of subject matter, although less austere, softer and less structural in composition than the Frenchman. Now and then Prokofiev would lead us quickly through a picture-filled gallery without pausing, saying, "This is academic."

We did stop for some time in a room with the huge painting by Ivanov of *Christ Appearing Before the People,* upon which he worked for many years in Rome. Imposing as this work is, more interesting to me was the vast amount of preparatory studies for it—figures, nude and draped in various poses, landscapes and fragments of landscapes, stones and grass, and many variations of the composition. Ivanov is an example of an artist who becomes completely obsessed with an idea, with subject matter, with a painting, like a minor Da Vinci with a *Last Supper.*

Then we came to the many rooms allotted to Surikov, Riepin, and Serov—painters of the middle nineteenth and early twentieth centuries. My favorite is the painter of Russian history, Surikov. He seems so Russian. He loved to paint snow and ice and cold weather and dark interiors with lighted candles in front of icons. His intense and deep identification with his subject matter lifts him out of the category of the usual dull historical painters. There is a sense of seriousness, dedication, in Surikov's work, of great effort, a feeling of grappling with difficult content and with almost insurmountable technical problems. His rooms, too, like Ivanov's, are filled with countless vivid studies for his complex compositions so densely packed with drama and action.

I found the work of Riepin extremely talented, but often lacking in taste and aesthetics. His exuberant naturalism became the model for much that is being done in Russia up to this day, just as Winslow Homer gave rise to the brand of the banal American school of seascape painting, which is still in vogue in the less sophisticated art communities in our country. There are at least two of Riepin's paintings, however, which are masterpieces of portraiture—one of the composer Anton Rubinstein with baton in hand; the other, a portrait of a dishevelled and bewildered Mussorgsky, painted a few days before the composer's death.

As for Serov, there seems to be in the Soviet Union today a predilection for him, a sort of cult, to the point of placing him above Riepin, who has long been considered the great Russian master. To me, however, Serov is simply a Riepin with a lighter touch, which is deceptively more modern, and perhaps for this reason is more satisfying to those who crave a less heavy-handed approach to art. Prokofiev pointed to a painting by Serov and said: "This is as good as a Manet." This comment, as well as others by several cognoscenti in Moscow, revealed a weakness in their critical evaluation of aesthetics. But on closer contact with these people I sensed a groping towards the more complex and sensitive values in contemporary art.

We had time only for a quick glance at the Soviet painting of today. There is a lot of lively realism. I liked a Hodleresque painting by Deineka and a few canvasses by Pietrov Vodkin, a very interesting painter who died in the thirties or forties. He was, apparently, the only artist who consciously based his work not on Riepinesque naturalism, but found his roots in the images of the old Russian icons.

I had an opportunity to talk about the problems of painting, to a limited extent, at the Dom Droozhbi—the House of Friendship—where, with Prof. Chegodaev as host, a few artists and writers came to greet me. I say "limited" because when I am called on to speak extemporaneously, the best ideas, what I really have in mind to say, come after the event. I spoke about the great danger that faces representational art —the loss of its utilitarian function to the new media for recording and describing events. I even projected the pessimistic thought that art, as we have known it, may not be compatible with our scientific age and may well be facing extinction. A symptom of this is the empty confusion of non-objectivism so widely promulgated today.

The Russians were more optimistic than I because from their point of view art still has a vital social function: that of propagandizing ideas and graphically presenting the goals of their society. They did not seem to be bothered by the doubts that beset me. In answer to this optimism I emphasized the hardship of the representational painter: the danger of being banal and pedestrian; the problem to find a new way of saying what has already been said before an infinite number of times; to add to art something that is expressive of our unusual era, so different from any other era in history. Representational art, I said, must constantly rediscover itself and renew itself to justify its continuation.

As I write this I am reminded of a conversation I had sometime ago with a contemporary poet whom I asked: "What is and what is not poetry today?" The simple answer has remained with me: "If one has read Ecclesiastes, Shakespeare, Keats, T. S. Eliot, etc., one realizes that all possible ideas have already been expressed. There are no new ideas. What may make poetry is a new way of expressing that which has already been said."

Our visit to the Pushkin Museum was guided by Chegodaev and three members of the museum staff. This museum is particularly proud of its collection of French Impressionist and Post-Impressionist art. Prof. Chegodaev pointed to the early Picasso of a circus girl balancing on a ball and murmured proudly, "This is the most beautiful Picasso in the world." The Cézannes took my breath away. I have seen many more Cézannes in the United States, but at the Pushkin Museum I found the choicest of all—the Harlequin and the Pierrot; a most "realized" self-portrait (like a green bronze); a very late small masterpiece, *Mt. Sainte-Victoire;* a monumental composition of a *Man at the Table;* and more landscapes and flowerpieces. The quality of this group made a deeper impression upon me than the profusion of Cézannes in the Chester Dale and Barnes collections. The finest paintings by Van Gogh, Gaugin, Matisse, Derain are found here. Also many strong and simple landscapes by Marquet. We were shown a unique collection of Fiume portraits, pictures of amazing vitality, as modern in spirit and feeling as any Roualt. Also there were rare examples of Egyptian sculpture.

The high point in the personal, friendly attitude of our guides to me, and through me to Americans generally, came when we were led into a room which Chegodaev called, "The Room of American Art in the Pushkin Museum." There was a good Mary Cassatt, several examples of Rockwell Kent, an Anton Refregier, a Gropper, a drawing by Alice Neel and, to my surprise, two old lithographs of mine.

"This is the only room in any European museum devoted exclusively to American art. We hope to enlarge and diversify it," said Chegodaev.

Then it became clear to me that the *idée fixe* of this quiet, patiently persevering man is to promote friendly relations between the Soviet Union and the United States through closer cultural, especially artistic, ties. He has already written a book on American art, and he dreams of exchange exhibitions of art of the two countries. Another hope of his which appealed to me very much is to have in Moscow an international exhibition of realism on the highest possible level.

I was also impressed by the staff members accompanying us, by their modesty and unpretentiousness. Occasionally they would comment intelligently on some painting or other. When one of them, an elderly woman, called our attention to a Zurbaran, Chegodaev said, "She just wrote a book on Zurbaran." It would be of interest here to mention how many books and monographs are written about artists in the Soviet Union. Almost all the people we met in the circle of artists have written books—on Velasquez, Gainsborough, Millet, Zurbaran, etc., and the young Prokofiev is at present working on a book about Manet. I saw some of their books. They are attractive without being lush, and I was told they are very popular and sell in large quantities.

Our visits to the homes of the artist Orest Vereisky, and Prof. Chegodaev where we met some of their friends, somewhat deepened our acquaintance with Russian intellectuals. In Vereisky's pleasant home, surrounded by a garden and tall birches (trees so sentimentalized in Russian literature), our charming hostess introduced us to Ludmilla Tolstaya, the widow of the famous novelist, Alexei Tolstoy. Before dinner we were joined briefly by Soifertis, a satirist whose water colors and graphics are sensitive in spite of their sharp and biting content. We had in common an admiration for George Grosz, and we talked about him. With Soifertis was his wife, the daughter of the well-known late Yiddish poet Quitko, one of the writers who perished in exile in the 1950's. Vereisky showed his work to all of us, and when I praised one of his drawings, he gave it to me.

The intellectual-pastoral setting of this house, the good food, the potent Armenian cognac, the lively conversation made this visit a memorable occasion. Mme. Tolstaya reminisced about her husband, we talked about his books and about his place in Russian literature today. In this warm and friendly company my halting Russian became more fluent, and I found myself using long-forgotten, appropriate proverbs. Later in the afternoon some more literary people dropped in, and the conversation continued in the same vein, comments on art and literature.

In Chegodaev's small apartment, filled with more than eight thousand books, the talk was centered on art, for we found ourselves in a group of artists and art historians exclusively. I leafed through monographs on the work of some of the artists present, and coming upon some reproductions of ballet dancers by our chief toastmaker, Pimenev, I was prompted to say, "You like Degas, don't you? He is my favorite artist, too." And I whimsically added: "He was the last Old Master." To which Pimenev replied in his deep, eloquent manner, "Not the last Old Master, the *first* modern master, whose new themes and new ideas inspired his contemporaries, those who came after him, and will continue to inspire future artists."

I was a little startled by this emphatic pronouncement of a rather accepted opinion, and said, "I agree with you, but Degas was a paradoxical man, and this is one of the paradoxes—he was the last Old Master, and a great new one."

Many toasts were made and downed to all present, even to two babies—to the grandson of the Chegodaev's, and to our grandson. Emboldened by Armenian cognac again, I talked freely, perhaps superficially, about tendencies and values in art in both our countries. Throughout this conversation there was in back of my mind the thought that I was perhaps expressing the usual glib and dogmatic opinions of Americans about contemporary Russian art. I felt in the artists there a disillusionment with their art of the last few decades which portrayed an optimistic heroism, and with their own present work still steeped in a naturalism which impedes its progress. I felt a restlessness, a groping toward some of the aesthetics and the refinements of Western art.

But what is it that Western art has for them? Is it abstract expressionism or any other kind of ephemeral "ism" that follows one another in quick and restless succession? Is the intrinsic value of this so-called avant-garde art greater than the intrinsic value of Russian art, platitudinous though it may be at this moment?

The formalism and stylism with which "Western" art is hoping to penetrate the Iron Curtain is foreign to and has little meaning for the Russians, is counter to their aesthetic tradition. Russian literature has always put the importance of content above that of style; and as for art (Lissitzky, Tatlin, Malevich, Kandinsky notwithstanding), its mainstream has always emphasized subject matter rather than style.

How well this thought was expressed by Boris Pasternak (who was embraced by the Western world for his artistry as well as for other reasons). In an interview with Olga Carlisle (*Writers at Work,* Viking Press, New York) he said:

I have never understood those dreams of a new language, of a completely original form of expression. Because of this dream, much of the work of the twenties which was but stylistic experimentation has ceased to exist. The most extraordinary discoveries are made when the artist is overwhelmed by what he has to say. Then he uses the old language in his urgency, and the old language is transformed from within.

Within the framework of this quotation contemporary Russian art can be criticized. It lacks the intense reaction to reality which alone can make traditional art living. For what the Russian artist is saying today is not what he is "overwhelmed" by, but what he is told to say.

Literature seems to fare better. Some writers are beginning to free themselves, according to Giacomo de Bendetti, an Italian writer from whose comments on this subject I quote:

Today the novel in socialist lands is being enriched with more complex, more intimate and psychologically deeper nuances. Authors approach men conscious of the entire complexity of life and feel themselves freed from their earlier aims to describe the fate of positive heroes only. Socialist realism today is more encompassing, more contemporary than it seems to the somewhat superficial Western judges.—*Literaturnya Gazetta,* Aug. 20.*

But then it is well known that Russian literature has always been on a more universal plane than Russian plastic art.

Eisenstein — Atasheva

We had an altogether unusual afternoon in Moscow, at the home of the widow of the great Russian film maker, Sergei Eisenstein. A former actress, she is known by her stage name of Pera Atasheva. Her small apartment is almost choked with memorabilia of her late husband. The walls are covered by shelves of books, and etchings by Pironesi, by Japanese woodcuts, a drawing by Picabia, an original poster of the film *Potemkin,* and numerous photographs of Eisenstein at different stages of his life. One of the two rooms is almost entirely devoted to the Eisenstein "archives."

Although Mme. Atasheva is now an invalid with failing eyesight and rarely leaves her home, she is devoting all the energy of her active mind to bring to greater public notice those aspects of her husband's talents and achievements not yet popularly known. At the time of our visit she was engaged in arranging an exhibition of Eisenstein's drawings in London's Victoria and Albert Museum, and asked us to contact Mr. Herbert Marshall there who is in charge of the exhibit. She also told us that Lincoln Kirstein is planning to bring this show to New York. We met in her house Valia Millman, an old friend of Pera and Sergei Eisenstein. This scintillating lady, also dedicated to the memory of the great film maker, is Mme. Atasheva's indispensable friend and almost daily companion.

We talked in English, which both ladies speak fluently. They are well acquainted with American literature, and have a great interest in Hemingway, an interest which is widespread in the Soviet Union. They also like the work of Faulkner and Salinger. On our way out, Valia Millman, who accompanied us, spoke with great warmth of her friend's indomitable spirit, of her interest in young people to whom her home and archives are always open. We left, feeling that we had visited a shrine to the memory of Sergei Eisenstein.

* My own free translation.

Leningrad

August 1963

ONE OF THE OBJECTIVES OF THIS TRIP WAS TO SEE AS MANY PAINTINGS BY REM-brandt as I possibly could, to look again at those I already know in Amsterdam, Vienna, the Louvre, and, with more expectation, to see for the first time those in Berlin, Dresden, and particularly those in The Hermitage of Leningrad. I have already touched upon some of them, but when I have seen them all I hope I shall be able to describe their cumulative effect upon me.

In Leningrad I went to visit the director of The Hermitage, Professor Levinson-Lessing, whom Renato Guttuso urged me to see. I found him frail and elderly with a sensitive face, altogether charming. He told me he has been with The Hermitage since 1921. I commented upon the excellent state of preservation of the old paintings, of their "genuine" appearance. I said I felt there was a minimum of tampering with them—to which he replied: "I'm glad you noticed that." From his tone I sensed he was really pleased by this recognition of the great care that is being taken of the paintings. We talked about contemporary art in America as well as in the Soviet Union. When I expressed my surprise that the Director of the old treasures of The Hermitage is also so keenly aware of what is going on in the world of art today, Levinson-Lessing answered: "For me art cannot be confined to things of the past only. For me it is ever continuing."

After he was called away, the conversation continued with the young art historian and assistant to the Director, Alexander I. Rusakov. He spoke specifically about the work that is being done in Leningrad. For some reason, he said, there is no outstanding painter in Leningrad, but the city has become the center for graphic art, with the old and esteemed Favorsky as its acknowledged master. There are printing workshops for lithography, etchings, woodcuts, conducted by the artists themselves. Exhibitions of these graphics have been held in various European cities, and even in New York.

From further conversation with Rusakov, I learned that his father, Isaak Rusa-

RAPHAEL SOYER

Levinson Lessing, director of the Hermitage in Leningrad.

kov, who died in 1952, was an artist also. He gave me a catalog with reproductions of his father's work, and I was surprised to find it artistic, sensitive, influenced by the French art of the fauve period. "Where are your father's paintings now? Are they known?" I asked.

"No, they are all in my house. My father had no success at all. He was unrecognized." I thought how sad and difficult it must have been for such a man to have lived at a time when brazen naturalism was in official vogue, and I expressed the hope that with the present tendency toward a re-evaluation of their art, painters like Isaak Rusakov may find a place.

In Leningrad besides the Hermitage there is the Russki Museum, devoted entirely to Russian art from the icon period to the present time, like the Tretiakovskaya Gallereia in Moscow. I was impressed by these two huge museums. They represent fully the work of their own artists from the very earliest time on. There is no mere sampling of so-called characteristic examples of their important artists, but rooms and rooms are set aside for Surikov, Riepin, Serov, Ivanov. Nothing so comprehensive can be found in our country. How good it would be to have museums in New York, Boston, Chicago solely for American art, with rooms dedicated to Eakins, Homer, Prendergast, George Bellows, etc.

We walked along the streets of Moscow and Leningrad, both quite different from other European cities. In Moscow its over-sized squares, its wide boulevards lined with newly planted trees and modern apartments, presented an almost discordant contrast to the old, narrow, crooked streets or *pereuloks,* with fenced-in courtyards and antiquated wooden buildings which are still found there. The section known as *Zamoskvaretchiye* (the other side of Moscow River, analagous to *Trastevere* in Rome) is particularly quaint, and not, as yet, so much affected by the changes brought about by modern city planning.

Of course the most striking spot in Moscow is the Red Square with the gilded cupolas and towers of the Kremlin behind the parapeted brick walls. I discovered that contrary to popular belief the name Red Square did not originate with the present regime. Centuries ago, when it was constructed, this square was named *Krasnaya Plostchad*—Beautiful Square, for *Krasnaya* means beautiful in old Russian, and it also means red. It is the most majestic square I have yet seen, with the whole length of the red-brick wall on one side, and the fantastic, colorful St. Basil's Church at the far end. In harmony with this architecture, and, as if growing out of the brick wall, is Lenin's Tomb, and an impressive aspect of this square is the long, patient line of thousands of reverent people waiting to visit this Tomb.

One morning, in a driving rain, we were taken by our guide to the Kremlin. The downpour did not deter the great numbers of people from thronging to see this place. Our guide kept close to us, and as we vainly tried to avoid the puddles that were filling the cobbled courtyard, we heard above the splashing of the rain our guide's voice dutifully reciting the history of the churches we were passing. When we

Monument to Peter the Great, Leningrad.

reached the Church of the Resurrection, the Oospenskie Sabor, we found our wet trek worthwhile. The walls, the ceilings and the columns were completely covered with religious frescoes of great simplicity and intensity. Without the usual paraphernalia that clutters up churches, the entire interior became a unique museum.

Before leaving Moscow, we walked around inside the Kremlin. It was late afternoon, the light was soft and clear. The ancient towers and the stony gray facades relieved by trees, gave the place a medieval charm.

On the way into Leningrad from the airport, we were struck by its difference from Moscow. There were comparatively few pedestrians, the traffic was less. There seemed to be an overall quiet, bordering on melancholy. That was our first impression, to be rather modified when we arrived at the center of town and found our hotel above a construction site where a new metro station was being built, the noisiest spot both day and night. As for people, we could see crowds of them from our window, going in and out of the metro station, and strolling, almost parading, after work along the Nevsky Prospect. Both in Moscow and Leningrad, by the way, one notices how straight the women walk, especially the young, like dancers.

Leningrad, that is old Leningrad, is very beautiful. It did not "just grow" like Moscow, but was planned and designed carefully on the style of a European city of that period, with long straight parallel streets and wide avenues. The Neva River and the numerous canals with bridges over them add to the city's unusual character. Delightfully pleasing is the architecture of the old low buildings with their flat or colonnaded facades in faded pastel shades of green, blue, orange, yellow—all with trims of white, brought in tone by the soft pearl-gray light which reminded us of the light on the islands off the coast of Maine. Here too, as in Moscow, the squares were large, well-proportioned. No parked cars marred their space and perspective, and the monuments were in keeping with the general architectural effect. The square with the equestrian monument to Peter the Great, which was made famous in Pushkin's poem as the *Medney Vsodnik* (The Bronze Horseman), is at the end of a park and faces the Neva River, and is particularly beautiful.

The greater part of our stay in Leningrad was spent in The Hermitage, but the most unforgettable of the few trips we took with our guide was to the mass cemetery of nearly a million civilians, victims of the long German siege of the city. Like all such places, it had its usual effect upon us: it filled us with anger and with sorrow. It is a vast area, a park with many lanes, and large mass graves, the smooth grass bordered with flowers, with a single headstone marked *1942* on each. We walked down the main path toward the monument at the far end, the figure of a woman symbolizing Mother Russia, standing tall in front of a low, gray, stone wall upon which is inscribed, in poetic prose, the epitaph to those buried there. Our walk was measured to the music of threnodies broadcast over the large field. Our guide's demeanor changed—she became silent, walked with bowed head, her lips pale and tightly compressed. Suddenly she exclaimed, with unexpected vehemence: "Nu, all right, Mr. Soyer. In wars soldiers kill one another. But does one have to do *this,* kill civilians and children, torture?"

Both Moscow and Leningrad seemed to us poorer in a material sense than other European cities. The window displays were meagre, the people's clothing, especially the men's, lacked the style and the well-cared for look one sees in the main streets of other European capitals. There were markedly fewer cars, especially in Leningrad. But both cities were abundantly stocked with books. Besides the many bookstores, there were stands and pushcarts on the sidewalks, in the middle of squares, and in their clean, spacious, over-ornate metro stations. These book displays were at all times surrounded by browsing, and buying, men, women, and even children. In one of these crowds, I overheard a young mother scolding her eight- or nine-year-old son, as she tucked his shirt in: "Nu, look at yourself, what an untidy fellow you are! I'll take your school books away from you if you don't take better care of yourself!"

Coming into the Soviet Union from western countries, one is struck by a sense of non-relationship of Moscow and Leningrad to the rest of Europe. Nor do the numerous tourists add to them the cosmopolitanism one finds in Rome, Paris, London. There seems to be a feeling of tense patience in the air, especially in Moscow, a seriousness in the faces of the people, as though weighed down by worry and responsibility. However, it may very well be that a visitor to New York could get a similar impression from the people in the streets and in the subways.

Rembrandt

August 1963

ONE MORNING IN THE HERMITAGE, I SIMPLY GASPED AT THE BEAUTY OF REMBRANDT'S *Prodigal Son*. It is golden, soft red, and deep brown. Time may have added its quality to it, mellowed the colors, hardened the paint into stone. Sensitive care has not destroyed these chemical changes which have become part of the painting. Standing in front of it that morning, I thought how unimportant and trivial discussions on aesthetics, abstraction, literariness in art can be. This painting defies such rationalizations. It is the most tangible, the most emotional painting I know, and it tells its story with deep eloquence. What keen and merciful observation Rembrandt must have had to be able to depict with such truth this meeting between father and son, the prodigal's head burrowing into the folds of the old man's clothes, and the old hands comforting with their touch.

These hands, and the hands in *The Jewish Bride,* symbolize for me the phenomenon of the old Rembrandt: his feeling for people, his acceptance of life and awareness and acceptance of death. How deep the sympathy in his portrayals of people; in his moving self-portrait as St. Paul; in the trembling gestures of the blind Homer and of the questioning St. Peter; and in the series of portraits of his son Titus, from the old-faced boy at his school desk (in Rotterdam) to the deathly pale young man (in the Rijksmuseum).

In the Hermitage there is also the *Danae.* The first thought that came to my mind when I looked at it was that here is indeed the antithesis to Giorgione's idealized reclining Venus, and to all the other elegant nudes ever painted. I ignored all the paraphernalia in this painting, and was hypnotized by this homely woman with her animated face, her big hands and soft belly, reclining, reaching out, her weight making a hollow in the bed clothes. It is truthful, touching, and human. One has to wait for a Degas to find again this profound treatment of a nude, though on a less epic scale, and without Rembrandt's unrestrained emotion. I must say here that I found Rembrandt's paintings in the Hermitage so delicately cleaned they were a joy to behold. They are not "scoured" as the paintings in England and in the U.S. seem to be. And for that matter it seems to me that the museums in Dresden, Munich, Vienna, Paris, Rome, Florence, Amsterdam, all know how to clean pictures without the ruthless tampering one finds in New York, Washington, and London.

Rembrandt's *Holy Family* shows his unique treatment of religious themes. It is not religious in the sense that the Italian and Flemish pictures are, it is simply a painting of a biblical story in a human setting, beyond any Dutch genre. Painted in his warm browns, reds and ochre, it has the feeling of peace and quiet, and the tenderness of a young mother watching over her child. The scene is not the usual manger or church found in other paintings of the Holy Family, but is an ordinary human dwelling. In the background, in deep shadow, is the Carpenter at work. Only the stiff angels in the upper left corner of the picture are indicative of any religious significance.

I imagined a gallery with Rembrandt's major paintings—the *Prodigal Son, The Jewish Bride,* the *Nightwatch,* the *Syndics,* the nudes of the *Danae* and of *Bathsheba,* his brooding self-portraits, *Saul and David,* the paintings in Brunswick, Stockholm and Kassel that I know only from reproductions—what a staggering impact a room like that would have! This work is not confined to time, and is beyond the borders of any place. No erudite historian can pigeonhole it, can adequately classify it.

Today there is (or there *was*—how ephemeral are these *isms!*) so much talk about "action" painting, about taschism, etc. One has to study the brush strokes on Saul's cloak; the way the paint is applied to the tablecloth in the *Syndics* and to the sleeve of the man in *The Jewish Bride;* the way the entire *Prodigal Son* is painted. The objectives of all the *isms* can be found there, and, of course, infinitely more—deep, human reality.

Amsterdam

September 1963

IN AMSTERDAM I RENEWED OUR ACQUAINTANCE WITH LEX HORN, WHOM WE HAD MET two years before, a serious painter and a stimulating, thoughtful person. We spent an interesting evening at his home, talking about the *isms* in art, about the life of artists in Holland where the government commissions painters and sculptors to decorate buildings, paint murals, and make monuments. Lex Horn told us that private sales of contemporary, native art are practically nil in Holland except for the work of those few who have attained an international reputation. It is the government's active interest in the arts which makes it possible for a man like himself to function as a painter, even though he is a well-known contemporary figure in Dutch art whose work is shown at The Municipal Museum of Amsterdam.

We went to his studio in a former schoolhouse which has been allotted by the city to several artists at a minimum rental. There is a number of such old buildings which the municipal government lets artists use as studios for very little money, provided they keep them in good repair. In this way the city of Amsterdam retains some of its fine old houses and at the same time provides artists with much-needed studios (New York, take notice!)

Horn showed us his work—landscapes, harbor scenes, streets and portraits, all done in a few years' time and showing developmental changes. There is a variety of influences—The French Fauves, Soutine, German expressionism, Kokoschka, Munch, leading up to recent semi-abstract trends. But basically, from the beginning, his work has had a strong expressionistic strain and his development has been a natural one, emanating mainly from within himself.

Before we left Amsterdam we had the pleasure of visiting the home of Ina Bakker, a Dutch ceramicist. She posed for me in New York when she lived there the previous winter, a charming and moody young woman who returned to Amsterdam with her American husband, the young scientist Michael Corner. He had a fellowship to study science at the University. We found them in a house so old it had to be propped up

Road to Calvary, by Rubens. (Amsterdam)

Dutch
painter
Lex Horn
Amsterdam

RAPHAEL
SOYER

Lex Horn.

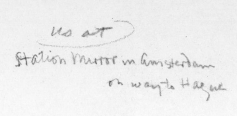

The artist and his wife waiting for a train in Amsterdam.

RAPHAEL SAYER amsterdam

From *The Jewish Bride*, by Rembrandt.

Sketch from Geertgen Lot Sint Jans. (Rijksmuseum, Amsterdam)

AMSTERDAM
1964

RAPHAEL
SOYER

REBECCA SOYER   EDITING "HOMAGE TO THOMAS EAKINS,
ETC."

Rebecca L. Soyer editing *Homage to Thomas Eakins, Etc.*

Ina and Michael Corner in Amsterdam.

RAPHAEL SOYER   Detail from Rubens, in Amsterdam

Road to Calvary, by Rubens. (Amsterdam)

Page from sketchbook.

with heavy beams. Their small apartment, with sloping floors and low windows, over-looked the canal at Prinsenkracht.

It was a still evening, the street lamps were lit and they and the trees and build-ings along the canal were reflected in the water. Upon the dark window panes, added to this mirage-like landscape, was the reflection of the lamp-lighted interior, like a montage. We relaxed with these people, enjoying the exotic food prepared by our hostess, the wine, and the animated conversation. A personal tone was added to our memories of Amsterdam.

Another interlude in our artistic wanderings was the visit to the home of an attractive Jewish woman, a widow, who bears a concentration camp number on her arm. She and her children are reconstructing their lives, not merely through the in-stinct for survival, but also with a strong social awareness to make a better life. From this family, as well as from Ina and Michael, we learned how the people of Amsterdam participated in our Freedom March to Washington, by staging a sympathy march of their own on the same day.

Hans, the fifteen-year-old son of our widowed friend, was packed full of all kinds of information, and told us about incidents of the underground in Holland during the Nazi occupation. One curious item relates to the finding of Hebrew words in the Dutch language. For instance, the Dutch word for prison is *Bayit,* which means *house* in Hebrew; the Dutch word for wild beasts is *Chayot,* which means *animals* in Hebrew. Hans told us about an inscription on the wall of a prison in which the anti-Nazi underground fighters were incarcerated: "In this Bayit there are no Chayot, but the finest men in Holland."

London

September 1963

COMING TO LONDON WE FELT AT HOME IN A BIG CITY AGAIN LIKE NEW YORK, WITH wide sidewalks and more controlled, although for us, confusing traffic. We loved the expanse of parks joining one another, and the many small squares filled with trees and flowers, and benches. One sunny afternoon we came upon a monument to Franklin D. Roosevelt in Grosvenor Square, in the middle of a terrace, surrounded by a low stone fence upon which were inscribed the Four Freedoms. We had a warm feeling of recognition. Flower beds brightened the terrace, and people were sitting on the stone steps and benches around the statue, enjoying the sun.

What a wealth of museums there is in London! We visited the National Gallery the very first afternoon, and looked again at the great paintings there: The Van Eyck portraits and the *Arnolfini Marriage;* the portraits by Petrus Christus, Van der Weyden, the *Master of Flemale,* and the religious compositions by Flemish masters; Holbein's *Ambassadors,* Durer's *Father,* Velasquez's early painting of *Christ in the House of Martha;* Rembrandt's portraits, one of which, *The Old Man in Red* resting on his elbow, seemed to have been recently overcleaned with lamentable results; the Titian group portrait of *The Vendramin Family in Adoration;* El Greco's *Agony in the Garden*—a strange composition of several paintings in one, eerie in color; the two Piero della Francescas; the Masaccio *Madonna,* the portraits by Lorenzo Lotto, the Bellinis, the Mantegnas, and many more. There are several huge rooms with more recent paintings: Ingres, Manet, Renoir, Cézanne, Pissaro, and a wall with paintings by Degas.

Degas

The wall of Degas at the National Gallery seems light and delicate in contrast to the symphonic paintings in Munich, Amsterdam, Leningrad. In the five canvasses on this wall can be seen the organic development of the artist. The early work, *The*

RACHAEL SOYER
from Titian in London

From *The Vendramin Family in Adoration*, by Titian. (London)

Pieta, by Michelangelo.

London
National
Gallery

RAPHAEL SOYER

Sketches from Velasquez and Rubens. (National Gallery, London)

Young Spartan Boys and Girls, always strikes me as unusually original in composition, in mood, and in drawing. I have always tried to understand this peculiar originality. It is true that he was influenced by Poussin, Ingres, by figures on a Greek vase. Yet there is about it this originality which I find difficult to explain. There is in it a youthfulness, combined with an ancient wisdom, a sunniness. Many changes are evident in this painting, corrections which Degas made no effort to hide, as though he were painting this picture just for himself. The group in the background is unfinished, tentative and fragmentary, which gives the painting an elusive quality of promise—it is not brought to culmination.

The *Femme Assise,* the portrait of a dark-haired woman, a gray-green shawl over her shoulders, seated in a red and white covered boudoir chair, is like a Vermeer with the addition of Degas' deep, psychological insight. This painting is ingeniously composed, full of abstract shapes.

With what amazing accuracy the *Acrobat Girl* is painted, hanging by her teeth under the vaulted dome in the circus. And the architectural background! One has to go back to Saenredam to find such sensitive and truthful rendering of this type of interior. If this comparison seems forced, it is certainly more reasonable and not so far fetched as that which links Mondrian to Vermeer and Saenredam.

Finally, the extraordinary painting, *Combing the Hair.* This is of the series of "women bathing, washing, drying, rubbing down, combing their hair or having it combed." It is a masterpiece of Degas' old age, painted roughly on rough canvas, with fauve-like breadth and almost a modern disdain for technical refinements. It is unusual in color, all red, the background, the robe, the hair. The figures and their living gestures, the mood of the entire painting, have the Degas precision and objective truth. Here Degas finally achieved the kind of universality and abstraction that comes only after a lifelong involvement with reality and human affairs.

The Tate Gallery

In the Tate Gallery there are a few more Degas, some Impressionists and Expressionists of various schools, and examples of all the international art movements of the last half-century. I was most interested this time in the English painting, to which the greater part of the Gallery is devoted. Of the early English school, two Hogarths—*The Heads of the Servants* and *The Shrimp Girl*—are unique in their directness and spontaneity. They seem commendably not "dated," fresh and unencumbered in comparison to what came soon after Hogarth. I have in mind Reynolds, Gainsborough, etc.

There are some visionary landscapes by Turner here. But in his desire to express the cosmic forces of nature, he often muddled around in a grandiose morass. Nor was I impressed by Constable—so naturalistic and fussy. I cannot uuderstand why he was admired by his great French contemporaries, Gericault and Delacroix. He was so inferior to their countryman, Corot.

In the Tate Gallery, as in other European museums, I noticed how fully represented were the native artists. There were rooms and rooms filled with pictures by Turner. There were many Constables, Hogarths, Reynoldses, and Gainsboroughs. A large room was devoted to pre-Raphaelite paintings. Of these I liked most two very early canvases by Dante Gabriel Rossetti, done at the age of twenty-one, which he never surpassed.

Of the more recent paintings I preferred the work of the lesser-known artists. For example, Gwen John's small, unostentatious, very personal portraits and figure studies, including an unusually perceptive self-portrait; Walter Greaves' *Hammersmith Bridge* —a positively unique painting of crowds of people watching a boat race. It is beautiful in color and pattern, and made me think of some early water colors of our own Prendergast.

There is a fine collection of the tasteful and intelligent work of Walter Richard Sieckert.

In a long hall devoted to contemporary art I found interesting the work of John Bratby, Joseph Herman, Lucien Freud, Jean Bratby, Peter Blake, some early, too sweet though, works of Victor Passmore, and a group of nightmarish pictures by Francis Bacon.

There is a very comprehensive collection of twentieth-century art representing artists of other countries besides England. There are also some very recent contemporary American paintings. In this respect the Tate Gallery is similar to the Museum of Modern Art in New York. Not all the pictures at the Tate are masterpieces of lasting importance, as its director, Sir John Rothenstein, admits. He convincingly states the reason for this in describing the function of the museum in his introduction to the publication *The Tate Gallery,* p. 52:

A gallery only of established masterpieces, skimmed off, as it were, from the art of their time, would be like a city whose every building was an architectural triumph that has alone been allowed to survive from among its fellows . . . . An understanding and a relish for any period, and of the classics of any period, would seem to demand at least an acquaintance with the period's ebb and flow . . . and accordingly with those works which fall short of being classics.

When we met Sir John Rothenstein at the Tate Gallery, our brief conversation revealed a person who, besides knowing the art of the past, has an enthusiastic interest in the many aspects of present-day art. He spoke with animation and warmth, and we got the impression that he makes it his business not only to know the work of the artists, but to have personal contact with them as well.

John Bratby

In London we met some of the people I visited two years ago: Peter de Francia, Joseph Herman, and John Bratby. Again John Bratby, both by his personality and by his work, captured my imagination. I vividly remembered the Bratby family which

I described in a *Painter's Pilgrimage* two years ago, and I looked forward to seeing them again in their extraordinary habitat in Blackheath.

The garden was more overgrown, and the house more neglected as a dwelling because the canvases seemed to have invaded the living quarters. Every room became a studio stacked with paintings and drawings, for they all paint—John, Jean, and their older boy of seven. I was surprised to find Bratby without his beard, having gained weight, and without that Dostoevsky look which had impressed me the first time I saw him. Now he looked much younger and his round, pink-complexioned face was completely unlined. His wife this time, friendlier and more outgoing, greeted me like an old acquaintance and stayed with us the afternoon.

Bratby himself was disturbed about some money and dealer difficulties, but when he began to show us his work his money worries seemed to disappear. He showed us a huge "mural" which he was commissioned to do for a Jesuit school. He wasn't being paid for it, except for the cost of the materials.

"I do it for nothing. I like to do murals, and I want to do more," he said. Like at our first meeting, I was moved by this total obsession to paint. The mural, propped against an entire wall of one of his studios, depicted the New Testament parable of the fish, in modern clothes. It was filled with many gesticulating, gaunt men and women with intense faces and convulsively begging hands, painted with feeling and vigor.

"I'm here five times," Jean Bratby said. Indeed, her dishevelled figure and her round, strangely beautiful eyes, were repeated in different spots of the canvas.

Back in the house, we saw many paintings of boats in several rooms, and in the hallways. "People here are fed up with my figure work, so I'm doing boats," Bratby said in passing. Jean shyly offered to show her work. In a room messed up with paintings and drawings, tubes of paint and rags, she pulled out canvases from behind chests and beds. Self-portraiture was the main theme, sensitive and searching, very often in shadow. Restlessly she began to look for some drawings, and for photographs of paintings, and soon gave up. She could not find them.

While John was out of the room, calling for a taxi for us, I asked his wife, "Was he always like this? I mean, did he always paint so much?"

"More so," she said. "When the baby would cry and I wanted to pick him up to comfort him, John would say, 'Leave him alone. Let's draw him crying.'" And there was an anxious look in her wide-open eyes. "Now he sometimes takes care of the garden."

"How does he manage to make so many paintings?" I asked.

"I don't know. I find him in the kitchen a lot, drinking coffee."

The next day at the Tate Gallery we saw the work of both Bratbys, both self-portraits, vividly revealing themselves in their environment: John painting in chaotic disorder, with his bewildered wife at his side; an extra pair of hands with paint brushes in the canvas, descriptive of his attitude to life, in which painting matters most.

This picture is called *Self-Portrait, Hands and Jean*. Jean's self-portrait is actually an image of herself in a mirror, as if confined within it, moody, in the reflected shadowy atmosphere of the room. Both paintings were outstanding in this room of contemporary British work.

Joseph Herman

Joseph Herman's invitation to visit him in his home in Surrey gave us an opprtunity to see the English countryside. The region is known as Thomas Gainsborough's country because he was born and painted there. That day was the most beautiful one during all our stay in England, sunny and warm. The house is an old, rambling stone one, set in very idyllic farm surroundings. We had lunch out-of-doors with Herman's family—his wife, a very handsome, stately young woman who is a doctor, and their two lively sun-tanned children, a six-year old boy and a sixteen-month-old baby girl.

Like many other artists, Joseph Herman has a collection of drawings and paintings, Pascin and Joseph Israels among them. Also a choice group of antique African sculptures. An old barn on the premises was converted into a fine, workable studio. He showed us his recent paintings which retain the content of the paintings I saw two years before: miners of Wales, in and out of doors, at work and at rest; interpretations of nature at its moodiest—evening scenes, sunsets with broody richness of color. Again I felt the early impact of Wales, of Permeke, and, at times, of Roualt, hang over his work. Their sonorous quality seemed to me almost oppressive.

I like Herman's exuberance and enthusiasm, his many plans for future work, his social awareness, and the intelligent way he talked about the art trends of our time. One of his comments was that the supposedly original and individualistic practitioners of the many current *isms* are really the conformists among the artists of our time because they all paint alike, all follow the fashionable trend and paint according to what is expected of them by those who wield power in the art world.

Peter de Francia

With Peter de Francia, the London painter, as a guide, we visited Hampton Court. There, besides some very good old masters—Titian, Holbein, Lorenzo Lotto—I saw the very early anonymous English paintings, portraits of ghost-like men and women in beautifully rendered costumes of the period, bejewelled and embroidered. They were almost abstract in the designs formed by the figures on the canvas, and in their featureless faces. They were dreamlike in color. These are the English paintings that fascinated me most.

Outdoors, the clear gray light unified even more the harmonious colors—the gray and the brick-red of the buildings with the richness of the flower beds in these

Joseph Herman.

famous gardens. Architecture-minded de Francia pointed out the stately beauty of the old stone buildings, and we were thrown into a poetic mood by the tranquility of the ancient courtyards.

Before leaving London we spent an afternoon in Peter de Francia's three-story house, where he lives, works, and stores his paintings. His work reveals his interest in the issues of our time: large, turbulent, exotic, and expressive canvases of struggling people.

Sergei Eisenstein

We acted upon Pera Atasheva's suggestion and wrote to Herbert Marshall, one of the men in charge of the Eisenstein drawing exhibition at the Victoria and Albert Museum. The response was prompt, with an invitation to visit him. We were greeted by a tall, exhuberant, pug-nosed Englishman. Inside the doorway, he pointed up to some broken beams in the ceiling, and said, "This house is the Last of the Mohicans of the Victorian Age. It's about to be demolished. We sold it and are moving to the country." This was in explanation of the genreal disorder around us. There was something unusual and unorthodox about Mr. Marshall's friendliness and informal hospitality.

"Come into the studio," he said, "I'll show you my wife's sculpture. She's Fredda Brilliant." The huge room with the double skylight was filled with skillful likenesses of Mayakovsky, Nehru, Krishna Menon, Pera Atasheva, and others.

Herbert Marshall studied with Eisenstein in Moscow for several years. He mastered the Russian language well enough to become a recognized translator of Mayakovsky. He gave us a book of his translations, and inscribed it to us.

Many people outstanding in various fields, such as poets, novelists, singers, also liked to draw. Among them were Pushkin, Victor Hugo, Mayakovsky, Caruso. From their drawings one can learn much about their personalities, their active minds. Sergei Eisenstein's drawings reveal his creative, imaginative, restless spirit, his sense of humor, his keen and satirical power of observation. These drawings are skillful, intense, rapid, urgent. Some of them are quite complex, with elements of cubism and futurism. A few are moody and delicately Picassoesque. Others remind one of Gauguin and Lautrec. This exhibition, which marked the fifteenth anniversary of Eisenstein's death, also contained his photos, letters and old clippings, and books about him. One poignant item was a page from a notebook upon which Eisenstein wrote in Russian: "Today I am fifty years old," signed and dated. This is exhibited upside down to show how his unique signature in this position resembles the battleship Potemkin. The day after Eisenstein wrote this, he died.

A Visit to the Burliuks

November 1963

WE VERY OFTEN TALK ABOUT THE BURLIUKS, WHAT INTERESTING AND UNUSUAL people they are; about their home on Long Island filled with pictures and books; their unusual habits; their complete devotion to art. Some friends of ours, newly come to art, wanted to meet the Burliuks, and drove us out to Long Island to see them, on a rainy after-Thanksgiving day.

As always, we were greeted very warmly by David and Marussia. Their faces lit up with genuine joy at seeing us, joy that is an outgrowth of many years' friendship. As always, we were impressed by the earthiness of these two old people, by the originality of their speech, their homey dress, their polite manner, the interior of their house crammed to overflowing with books, pictures, and sculptures; their huge home-made table, roughly fashioned by their vigorous sculptor son from a tremendous tree trunk split in half, planed and polished with use into a smooth, almost silky finish, and resting on short tree stumps for legs.

Immediately after the ceremonial greetings they offered to take us to their "gallery," about a quarter of a mile from their home, a simple structure of cinder blocks, built to house the many pictures collected and painted by David Burliuk. During the summer months it is open to the public under the direction of Marussia Burliuk, who takes pride in having brought the "museum," as she calls it, to Hampton Bays.

It was still raining hard, and Burliuk put on an ancient gray herringbone tweed overcoat, which beautifully enveloped his aged figure. It had stains of green paint, thinned by time, which, on the yellowed gray of the coat, looked like moss on earth.

In the "gallery" Burliuk showed us paintings by many artists and also his own work. After he set up a whole line of his own vigorous and colorful pictures, he suddenly walked away to the far side of the gallery, where he sat down on a chest, as if to rest, and for a while seemed to become oblivious to the activity at the other end. Mrs. Burliuk took over showing the pictures. To the great and unexpected delight of the Burliuks, our friends bought a painting. After this we went back to the house.

110

D.D. BURLIUK.

Raphael Soyer 1964

David Burliuk.

Marussia Burliuk.

On the oaken table there soon appeared quantities of bread and cheese, wine, vodka and tea. The conversation became very lively. Burliuk was in an unusual merry mood and held forth loudly and eloquently. Every once in a while he was interrupted by Marussia in Russian. "Father, stop hollering. You're not a priest in a church." Whereupon his face would assume an expression of sweet condescension, and he would say to his audience, "Dear Marussia tells me not to talk so loud."

He told us about his art in the days of the *Blaue Reiter,* describing Kandinsky to us; the melodramatic days of Futurism in St. Petersburg and, of course, talked about Mayakovsky. Burliuk loomed big in these reminiscences. He was boastful, exultant at his long life.

"I almost died last winter," he said at one point. "But you know who did it for me? Georges Braque!"

I was glad to have taken my sketch book. I made a drawing of Burliuk talking, with one hand raised in a posing gesture; wine, bread, and books on the table, and pictures on the wall. I sketched Marussia Burliuk, her limpid eyes and dishevelled hair, while she was animatedly talking to my wife about our recent visit to Leningrad and Moscow. This wasn't all. A huge guest book appeared, in which we all had to write personal comments, and I doodled in it and in other books and catalogs. Before we left we exchanged presents.

Homage to Eakins

February 1964

I'M FINALLY AT WORK ON THE LARGE VERSION OF HOMAGE TO EAKINS. I HAVE MADE for it ten preparatory portraits from life: also three group compositions in various stages of completion. In the past year I examined and studied group portraits by Rembrandt and Franz Hals, as well as compositions by Veronese, Caravaggio, and, of course, Fantin-Latour. In one of the Skira books I came across a painting by the Spaniard Solana, a simple and direct composition consisting of a long, rectangular table with men seated along both sides, like Franz Hals, but without his gusto, exuberance, movement. It influenced me in planning my work. Its stillness, I felt, would be suited for my composition. I made a sketchy drawing of this painting from the Skira reproduction. My canvas with the *Gross Clinic* in the background has to be vertical, whereas the Solana is horizontal in position.

When the large canvas was brought up into my studio I was appalled by its size and by the raw whiteness of its surface. For two weeks it stood propped up against the wall without my approaching it, as if I were trying to ignore it, to pretend it wasn't there. I busied myself with other canvases. Finally I tinted it with the same ground which I used for the single portraits and preliminary studies, the same preparation of white, yellow ochre, and cobalt blue diluted in turpentine. Unfortunately, this canvas did not take the preparation as well as the others did because they were more absorbent. This one was smooth and began to look like a blotchedly-painted wall. I was quite dismayed by it and even thought of stretching another huge canvas of a different texture. But finally I decided to use this one after all.

As soon as I began I was immediately confronted by the following problems (which, frankly, I had anticipated): On the large canvas I had to make the figures on the first plane, in the foreground, somewhat bigger than life, the size I painted them in the preparatory studies, so that the figures in the back should not appear too

114

Preliminary sketch for *Homage to Thomas Eakins.*

Sketches from *The Women Guardians of Haarlem Almshouse*, by Frans Hals.

small. But the main difficulty I found to be copying my own work. I was amazed by what had gone into the making of the portraits, how meaningful each seemingly haphazard brush stroke was, how expressive was every varied patch of color. These were not definitive studies that could be accurately transferred to the final composition; they lacked absolute rendition. They were tentative, nervous, personal, calligraphic, immediate reactions of the artist to his subject. They became art works in themselves rather than functional studies for a larger work. And therefore difficult to copy. But I did copy them, realizing at the same time that it was impossible to maintain the spontaneity of the sketches, to copy each brush stroke as it was done originally, almost automatically.

May 1964

I have been working on the big canvas for months now, but not every day. Sometimes a week goes by without my even glancing at it. During this time I have finished about half a dozen other paintings, one of them a double portrait of John and Alice Rewald in their home, with the statue of the skirted Degas ballet dancer in the background. Another one, a small head of John Rewald, for which he uncomfortably sat in a hard chair in my studio. While he was posing, I threw out the thought that I might want to include his portrait in the large Eakins composition. (Like Ingres, in his *Apotheosis to Homer,* I wanted to include all those for whom I have regard, for one reason or another, and I admire Rewald for his work on the Impressionists and Post-Impressionists. Rewald said, "I really don't belong among American painters in *Homage to Eakins,* but if you want to put me in, you may." And then he added in his somewhat dry, professional manner, "It's *your* Grande Jatte."

He interests me, this writer on French art, this lucid, factual art historian, who on occasion is definite and personal in his opinions, if unobstrusively so. His extraordinary histories made the art epoch about which he writes real and alive to me. I felt almost in physical contact with Courbet, Manet, Renoir, Degas, Cézanne, Monet, Pissaro, Seurat, Van Gogh and Gauguin, as well as with the lesser personages of that milieu.

I was not completely successful in my portrayal of this chain-smoking, restless cosmopolitan with the worried blue eyes. It was difficult to get the ever-changing mobility of his face. He never looked the same for any length of time.

"I influenced a collector to buy an Eakins, a painting of children at play," he said, showing his regard for Thomas Eakins.

The canvas does not loom so unwieldy and big as it did upon its arrival. It seems to have been shrinking while I have been filling it with one figure after another. I am following the original plan of the first preliminary composition with this change: in the first study the *Gross Clinic* painting is right in the center of the background, so that the head of Dr. Gross is directly and awkwardly above the head of Lloyd Good-

Mr. and Mrs. John Rewald. Sketch for painting.

Small version of *Homage to Thomas Eakins*. (Unfinished state.)

Detail from a life study of Henry Varnum Poor.

rich. To correct this I moved the Clinic painting slightly to the left on the big canvas. Also, as I added more figures, I found it necessary to reshuffle the group from the original positions in the preliminary study.

Besides the *Gross Clinic,* there are parts of two other smaller paintings of Eakins in the background, one on either side of it—the *Salutat* and the *Sculptor Rush in His Studio.* My first sketch for the composition, with just a few figures around the table, had the portrait of Whitman and Eakins' self-portrait on either side of the clinic.

June 1964

The canvas is all covered. All the figures and faces are at last painted in their first state. I found a place for my self-portrait, for which I had made three studies in different positions on one canvas. I have also indicated a figure of a woman serving a tray with drinks, for which my daughter promised to pose. Now and then when I step back to look at this painting, I find it rather impressive. The composition seems to satisfy me. But it's a long way from being finished.

My goal is to make the whole painting as living and intense as each individual portrait of the artists. Will I be able to capture the tremor in the temples of Jack Levine's portrait, the anxious face of Moses Soyer? Or the aura of aloneness about Hopper? However, although I have hardly begun to dig into these portraits, their being next to one another seems to help to point up their individual likenesses.

It got around that I was doing this group portrait of the artists, and people frequently ask me how it is getting along. This worries me. It is still in its initial state, and its final realization is questionable. I am never certain of a painting until the very last brush stroke is applied. About this particular one I have often a very uneasy feeling that I simply am struggling with something beyond me for which I have not enough technical knowledge. Such paintings are not done today. The secret of doing big group paintings has been lost. Probably Fantin-Latour and Eakins were the last portrait painters of this type. It is impossible to paint that way now. The portraits painted today are fragmentary, personal, capricious, nervous, tentative. They are incomplete, accidental, at times full of inaccuracies. But they are fascinating—revealing the artist more than the subject he paints. If ever completed, my painting should have some of these characteristics.

Homage to Thomas Eakins.

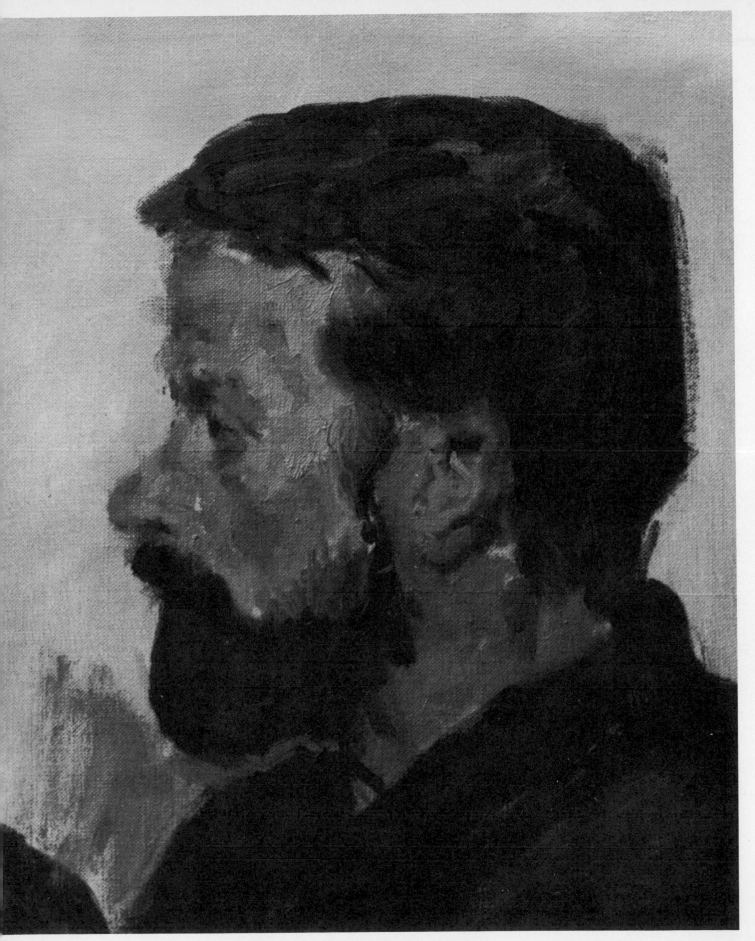

Detail from a life study of John Dobbs.

Detail from a life study of Moses Soyer.

Detail from a life study of Lloyd Goodrich.

Detail from a life study of John Koch.

Detail from *Homage to Thomas Eakins.*

Detail from *Homage to Thomas Eakins*.

ANTONELLA DA MESSINA
MUNCHEN

1963

RAPHAEL
SOYER

master of
Flemalle

The Portrayal of the
Negro in American Painting

July 1964

ON THE WAY TO VINALHAVEN WE STOPPED AT THE ART MUSEUM OF BOWDOIN COL-
lege in Brunswick, Maine, to see the exhibition, "The Portrayal of the Negro in
American Painting," a chronologically arranged historical selection of paintings,
from colonial times to the present. Some of the paintings depict the events in the life of
the Negroes in the United States, such as slave market scenes, the visit of the Mistress
to the Negro quarters (a Winslow Homer), Negroes at work, and early portraits of
distinguished Negroes. The better pictures are simple genre scenes of Negro home life,
like the water color by Thomas Eakins of a barefoot Negro boy dancing to the music
of a guitarist, and an unostentatious study in oil of the same boy; also *Shooting Quail*,
another Eakins water color as well as the *Masquerade Party* by Winslow Homer, his
charming *Boy with Sun Flower,* Haveden's *Their Pride and Joy,* and Andrew Wyeth's
painting of an old man and his granddaughter.

Among other painters was Alexander Brook, whose *Georgia Jungle* I hadn't
seen for many years—a gray and brown landscape of scrawny, leafless trees and Negro
shacks reflected in muddy puddles, and in the foreground some gaunt Negroes. Also
Joseph Hirsch's *Lynch Family* and Jack Levine's *Birmingham 1963,* which was
especially timely. Jack Levine told me that for three months he worked exclusively on
this painting.

I was gratified that my painting, *City Children,* which included a Negro boy,
was so well hung and looked so well. This is the kind of painting I do from time to
time which leaves me uneasy because it is open to accusations of sentimentality. This
particular one is of an actual scene I witnessed in front of a New York tenement of
three somewhat melancholy children together physically, yet disassociated from one
another.

130

I left a note for Marvin Sadik, the young curator of the Museum, expressing my admiration for the painstaking research that must have gone into the preparation of this show, and praising it for its timeliness and excellence. Such an exhibition, I wrote in the note, should be circulated throughout the country.

Vinalhaven

July-August 1964

MY LANDSCAPES OF VINALHAVEN ARE REALLY MORE LIKE STILL LIFES. I START OUT with the idea of making a landscape, but invariably it becomes still-life-like. Perhaps it's due to the content I choose—gray rocks, abandoned piers with their debris, piles of weathered lobster traps—excellent still-life material. Only a small part of the canvas is allotted to sky and that is gray and flat. The entire lanscape gradually turns gray even if it is started on a sunny day since gray days predominate on the Island.

The aspect of these canvases, then, is such that they could very well have been painted in a studio, under a skylight. The fact, however, is that I do paint them out-of-doors. Intrinsically I am not really interested in light effects, but in the foreground perspectives, in the shape and texture of rocks, in the architecture of the piled-up traps, in the depth of bushes, and in the contour of leaves when they enter into the landscape.

I am conscious of the fact that I'm one of the very few now who paint directly from nature with their easels and canvases out in the open. This was the method of Pissaro, Monet, Cézanne and Van Gogh, and of Courbet, too. I enjoy it. I feel the air and the wind, and once in a while I hear the sound of a jet plane, and it amuses me that while I am down here making a picture with the age-old tools of brushes and paints, there are satellites hurtling in space.

Vinalhaven, naturally picturesque and once a thriving and vigorous community, has acquired a peculiar charm that semi-abandonment and isolation give. It is the largest of the Fox Islands in Penobscot Bay, an hour and a half by boat from the mainland. When it was one of the busiest granite-quarry centers in the country it was thickly populated. There is no granite mining now; the quarries have become swimming holes, and the chief and almost only occupation has become fishing for lobster and herring. The young people leave the Island, the old ones stay on, and when they die their houses are left empty, soon to deteriorate and fall apart, unless bought and

BRUD
CLAYTER
VINALHAUEN
MAINE

RAPHAEL
SOYER

Brud Clayter.

restored by summer people. There are stretches of jungle-like wasteland, with gray remains of wooden houses showing through the trees here and there.

However, there is a well-organized township, and along the harbor, starting from the newly-built ferry landing, the old Main Street with its fish factory, power plant, post office, and the usual stores is still the center of activities. There are two or three churches, a movie house, two school buildings, and a new medical center.

Among the summer people are a few sculptors and painters, but there is no obstreperous art colony. The island does have an art tradition—Marsden Hartley spent several summers here with his friend, the poet Harold Vinal, now aging and semi-blind; and Gaston Lachaise as well as John Marin are said to have worked here.

I became acquainted with a local painter, Brud Clayter, born and bred on the Island. In his adolescent years he was ill, and although his ailment was finally cured, it left him with a ravaged physique and a heightened sensitivity. He paints delicate water colors and admires strongly the work of Andrew Wyeth and Edward Hopper. In a recent water color he depicted a solitary house in a hayfield.

We spend time together—he brings me work to criticize, and we talk about art, literature, politics, and life in general. He sometimes reminisces about what happened on the Island when he was a child. One of the incidents he witnessed about thirty years ago sounds, as he tells it, almost like a folk story out of Tolstoy: A seven-foot skeleton of an Indian found in a grave on a wooded hill was to be viewed by an anthropologist from the State University. While people were waiting around the open pit for the expert to arrive, "the meanest and pushiest man in town," wanting to be first at the scene, rowed his boat frantically to the foot of the hill, rushed pantingly up, elbowed his way through the crowd, and dropped dead into the grave onto the skeleton, smashing it to bits.

Mauricio Lasansky

There is one summer resident on Vinalhaven whom I must mention, the graphic artist Mauricio Lasansky. He has installed a real workshop with all the necessary equipment, light and machinery in an old house overlooking a particularly isolated and picturesque cove on the Island.

For the last three years Lasansky has been engaged in chronicling the Nazi atrocities in a series of twenty-five over-sized drawings done in pencil and water-color. He calls these emphatically "The Nazi Drawings." When I visited him last he showed me some of the still unfinished compositions, a group of intensely expressionistic drawings, gruesome, shocking and brutal—a sort of neo-realism familiar today. This work, however, has validity and purpose, exonerating it from possible accusations of sheer necrophilia and sadism.

The size of the drawings, the sparse medium of pencil with touches of dull water-color tints, the irony of using pages torn from the Bible, indiscriminately collaged as

Mauricio Lasansky.

a background, and the repetition of a tattooed concentration camp number, haphazardly stamped on the surface, all create a strong, new impact. A few drawings deal accusingly with the role of Pope Pius XII, a face and figure cringed with fear and remorse.

Coming out of the studio into the relentless sunshine (the Island had been suffering from a long drought) I had to make an effort to free myself, like one awakening from an evil dream.

Jack Levine

August 1964

IN THE OGUNQUIT MUSEUM WE SAW A SMALL BUT QUITE COMPREHENSIVE RETRO-spective exhibition of the work of Jack Levine to which again I responded, as I always do, with heightened interest. For sheer painting ability, he is one of the most vigorous painters in America today. By comparison, the other paintings in the Museum seemed anemic and tame.

To begin with, there were some remarkable Ingresesque drawings, some of them dating back to his early teens. The earliest painting shown here, which I have never seen before, was one of three men playing cards, painted when he was not quite twenty years old. Interestingly enough, it lacked the usual naive charm one associates with youthful work. It had instead an overall soberness of an older painter.

The other paintings familiar to me seemed even more striking than I remembered them because they were displayed under better-than-usual conditions in a spacious room with excellent light: a few early conversation pieces in dark-red and slate-black, of grotesque men; *The Passing Scene,* a tableau of an old man and child, a fantastically-rendered old workhorse, a black sky, old tenements, clotheslines, debris with a fragment of a foreign language newspaper. Chagall, Sholem Aleichem, the early George Grosz, came to mind. But this was different. There was no folklore or humor. It was grim, yet compassionate, not satrical. It was painted in tangible terms, yet it had a strange echo quality. It recalled the immigrant era.

Among other paintings were the powerful composition of *Cain and Abel;* the well-known *Medicine Man* (on loan from the Metropolitan Museum); the sombre painting of the execution of a Spanish Loyalist; and the politically biting depiction of Parnell Thomas of infamous memory, stabbing Legislature in the back. There were also the humorous satires often characteristic of Jack Levine, the pathetically sentimental, garish couple of the *Black Freighter,* the pleasantly soft Eve with her constitutionally inadequate Adam, and finally the unique self-portrait—a pale, pre-

137

Detail from a life study of Jack Levine.

cocious young artist being chucked under the chin by a ponderously floating Rubensesque naked muse.

This self-portrait made me think of Levine as I first knew him in the early 1940's. He must have already been well-known then, for he was among the portraits I painted of eminent artists—Sloan, Weber, Marsden Hartley, and others. I remember him in my studio, quiet, pale, with thick, heavily-rimmed glasses, "a veritable Shostakovich," Nick Cikovsky said of him when he too saw him that day. Since then I have begun to know him somewhat better. I privately place him, however, in the category of those whom, because I admire them, I shy away from knowing as intimately as I think I could know them. I had this feeling toward Guy Pène du Bois, who was my teacher, and later toward Kuniyoshi, Hopper, and a few others.

While he was posing for the Eakins group, Jack Levine was silent, grim, immovable. The first sitting ended in complete failure, and left me dejected. "I'll have to do it all over again, on a different canvas," I said gloomily. "I'll need a couple of more sittings." He agreed without question.

The second attempt was more successful. This portrait is the most poignant and satisfying of all the studies for the Eakins painting. I think I caught his tenseness, the intellectual brooding in his blue eyes under the thick lenses, the mobility of his features.

Jack's studio is the messiest, the most uncomfortable I have ever seen. He comes there just to paint. "I can't even get a drink of water here," he says. There is no sink in his studio. I remember a winter afternoon when I visited him. There was a harsh overhead light. A huge canvas on an easel threw a thick black shadow on the wall. There was a model stand, with a great heap of cloths on it. On the floor, or perhaps on the stand, was a whiskey bottle. There were some art books on crude shelves. One of the walls was discolored and scaly from a chronic leak. Not a painting was on the walls, just a few photographs clipped from newspapers, one of a sanctimonious, well-known churchman fondling a baby who was bawling in his face, and others of similar tone.

The painting table was piled with used up, but not discarded, paper pallets; with quantities of paint tubes, half-squeezed ones mixed with new ones; and with huge short-handled brushes of the kind used by house painters. When I expressed surprise at the size of the brushes, he said, smiling wryly, "Essentially, I am an action painter," and he pointed to the large semi-nude on the easel, which was painted with tremendous vigor and contained all the gusto, and more, of action painting plus, of course, the content—a young girl in the pose of a Medici Venus, but clutching a slip in front of her body.

He was at that time involved with a series of pictures on the mythological subject The Judgment of Paris. Again there was satire—the old theme in modern dress—chorus girls in burlesque semi-attire with fantastic hats and hairdos, with their agents and pimps "in black tie" in a hubbub of bank buildings, automobiles and neon lights. "I am a satirist, as you see," he said.

But then he showed me other paintings: a gentle and sympathetic study of a young model; a charming portrait of his daughter, and a directly painted head of Ruth Gikow.

He talked about technical matters of painting, various media, effects of one layer of paint upon another, glazings, etc. He was articulate and knowledgeable, but it was hard for me to follow, since my mind doesn't work that way. I have never given too much thought to such technicalities. What never ceases to fascinate me about Jack Levine is his mental alertness, his extraordinary talent, and the seemingly inexhaustible reserve of ideas for paintings to come.

Paris

August-September 1964

PARIS THIS YEAR HAD SOMEHOW A GREATER IMPACT ON ME THAN ON THE PREVIOUS visits to it. The weather was particularly fine, the day was clear and sunny as we found ourselves in the planned vistas outside the Louvre. The epic paintings, so heroic in size and spirit, by David, Ingres, Gericault, Delacroix and Courbet, are to me the glory of France. Again I felt that Delacroix never surpassed his early *Liberty Leading the People* and *The Massacre of Scio,* although he remained a great painter until the end of his life. And the three paintings of Courbet, the *Wave,* the *Studio,* and the *Burial* are enough to make anyone immortal. The *Studio,* mural-size though it is, has the intimacy and quality of easel painting at its unsurpassed best.

In a section of the Louvre we saw a large and well-displayed exhibition of Rouault. He painted in a continuous mood of poetic exhaltation, but he is one of those artists, such as Van Gogh and Dufy, who have no personal hold upon me, brilliant and profound as they may be. The obviousness and the repetitiousness of their spectacular styles become monotonous.

I went with the artist Joseph Floch to an exhibition of the travelling Johnson Wax Collection, known as "Art: U.S.A." at the Musée d'Art Moderne. It was the usual type of contemporary painting one can find in Europe and America. More than three-quarters of it consisted of pictures in what is now rapidly becoming known as the "international style." In other words, they are all alike, no matter where they are painted—in New York, Amsterdam, London, Buenos Aires, or Tel-Aviv. These happened to be American paintings, most of them huge in size, "freely" painted, noisy in color, and themeless. Some were "absolutely idiotic," Joseph Floch said. There were representational pictures, too, but they seemed exasperatingly modest and were lost in the pandemonium.

"Even if there were a Cézanne here, no one would see it," remarked Floch. These "internationalists"—I am always amazed at their lack of artistic reticence, their al-

141

Israeli artist in Café Coupole.

Leopold Levi, old Paris painter.

old Paris
painter

Pink
face

intensely
pink eyes
loyish on one

Leopold Levi
Paris

most hysterical clamor for attention, so obvious in the contentless gigantism and preposterous color of their canvases.

How different are the paintings at the Jeu de Paume, which I visited that same morning—quiet, serious, honest, workmanlike. Unforced, without public approbation in mind. Especially so Degas. He did not care at all for the opinions of the critics, the cognoscenti, the museum directors, and the public. He simply painted in a way that pleased him. He was his own severest critic. Very often he made revisions in composition and corrections in drawing long after the paintings were finished, and did not bother to cover them up. Thus in the group of girls in the *Jeunes Spartiates* in London's National Gallery, he changed the position of the legs without painting out the original ones, leaving an extra number of legs. This gives his work an added fascination for me because it creates an element of tentativeness and even of movement that brings a hint of futurism to mind. Some parts of his canvases are finished with the most delicate completeness, while others are left in the rough, strangely enhancing them.

Two of Degas' great paintings in the Jeu de Paume are *The Absinthe Drinkers* and the *Repasseuses*. The first one is the quietest, even the drabbest painting I know. It is all in nondescript black, white, gray, some yellow ochre, with a touch of light green of the absinthe. Yet this poverty of color adds to the deep and hypnotizing effect this picture always has on me. The relegation of the two withdrawn people to one side of the canvas accentuates the mutual loneliness which gives this picture its strong psychological bent. It is as unique in its way, as is *The Arnolfini Couple* by Van Eyck. It brings to mind the monochromatic paintings of Louis Le Nain.

The *Repasseuses*, on the other hand, is colorful. Every tint adds to the reality and originality of this masterpiece. It is painted on the raw, unsized surface of the canvas with the most subtle economy of means. Every brush stroke is functional. Against all rules of art esthetics, Degas tackles such unorthodox subject matter as a woman yawning and transcends its literary and anecdotal aspect by means of great simplification of form.

I met in the Louvre Abraham Chanin, art historian and lecturer at the Museum of Modern Art of New York. In a room most of which was filled with very capable but mechanical French eighteenth-century portraits, he was studying a group of small, modest still lifes and genres by Chardin. With great relish he pointed out to me the textural and paint qualities in these canvases: "Look at the reflection of the apples in the silver goblet."

Later we took a walk to the Rue St. Denis section. "It's like Fourteenth Street as it used to be," Chanin said. Bars and cafes filled the wide street, and prostitutes mingled with the customers. In doorways of narrow, dark streets there were groups of cosmeticized, frizzed girls. Some were charming and young. Older ones, bitter and tough-looking, wore tight leather dresses, their breasts and bellies accentuated by the

Abraham Chanin.

light shining on them. "They look like the Maillol nudes in the Tuileries, lit by the sun," I said.

Interesting as well were the gray, shabby, scaly houses which seemed to be crumbling. Some unsafe, ancient buildings had been demolished, exposing a whole area of windowless walls. "These walls are straight out of Daumier!" exclaimed Chanin, "and these old gray buildings, you can see them in the background of Delacroix's *Liberty Leading the People.*"

But the high point of our stroll was the little Park of the Innocents. "Ironic," said Chanin, "a park with such a name in this section of slums and prostitutes." This park was reserved only for the neighborhood mothers and children. We went there to look at what served as an inspiration to the young, impressionable, avid Renoir. The attendant allowed us to enter and there in the center of the Park, on a strange polygon structure, were the bas-reliefs by Cojon of sensuous, yet innocent, semi-draped female forms. They were sparklingly clear, having been recently cleaned, like other monuments and buildings, by the order of Malraux. While we were admiring these we were also aware of the women and children, obviously from this slum area. The older children noisily circled around us, boldly touching us in their bid for attention.

Life was teeming and complex, real. I felt more than ever that it is the basis of all art.

Joseph Floch

Joseph Floch invited me to his "wonderful" studio: "I have a model, and you and I will draw for a few hours. It's much quieter and nicer here than any of the studios we had in New York."

I took my sketch book, its hard, blue covers worn and yellowed from being carried in my hands these many weeks. It was not Floch's permanent studio, it was just rented for the summer, but it already had all the characteristics of any place where he happened to be working—neat, clean-swept, the cot and the wall above it covered with woven fabrics of South American design. No paintings or drawings on the whitewashed walls. So unlike my own work rooms which generally become messy, their walls covered with sketches, half-finished canvases and reproductions clipped from magazines and newspapers. I remember in one studio how Arshile Gorky looked about him and said in his usual melancholy voice, "Gee, you still have a romantic life with pictures!" I didn't exactly know what he meant then, but that phrase has remained with me. To try to explain it now would be too much of an inquiry into Arshile Gorky.

Floch was absent-minded, didn't seem particularly interested in drawing, but fussed around with canvases which had beginnings of compositions. He made only half-hearted attempts at drawing from the model, not caring what the pose was. I had the feeling that he engaged the model that morning for my benefit, for he knows well

Café in St. Michele, Paris.

Café Coupole, Paris.

how much I love to draw. As on many other occasions, I was grateful to him for this particular attention.

After the model left we spent the rest of the afternoon talking about art and literature, and also about music, with which Joseph, like many other Viennese, is well acquainted. We discussed particularly the drawings of George Grosz, Pascin, and Schiele. Among other things I remember Floch saying that these three, although labelled Expressionist, went beyond this, or any other, classification:—"They invented personal styles through which they expressed the dreams, the sufferings, the anxieties of life."

He found parallels for these artists in literature and music—the sensuousness and gaiety of Pascin in Offenbach, the cruelties and anxieties of George Grosz and Schiele in Kafka.

For many years Joseph and I were close neighbors in the Lincoln Arcade, lately demolished to make way for the newly risen cold, prophylactic, transparent buildings of Lincoln Center. This skillful and poetic painter would often quote from the Bible, from Goethe, Heine, and Tolstoy. We would see each other many times a day, show each other our canvases in all the stages of their completion, criticize each other honestly if delicately, work together from the same models, pose for each other. How often our long talks would help to clarify our artistic aims within this bewildering and confusing world. Our contacts now are mostly telephonic since we have become geographically separated in our monstrous, complex, city.

Musée d'Art Moderne

At the Musée d'Art Moderne I again felt the intimate warmth of the two last impressionists, Vuillard and Bonnard. Bonnard especially was fascinating in color and in his absolutely personal simplicity of drawing. His composing, too, was very original in the way he placed figures in the immediate foreground of landscapes, resulting in an almost surrealistic illusion of space, with the pure Bonnard color binding earth, sky and figures together in a living way.

Here I discovered another "Homage" painting, this one to Cézanne by Maurice Denis—a group of artists and critics including Bonnard, Serusier, Vuillard, Valloton, and Denis himself, with a still life by Cézanne on an easel. It was rather dull—a horizontal row of woodenly-painted heads near the top of the canvas, the rest of the painting consisting of their black-clad figures.

Suzanne Valladon's paintings stood out by their directness, good drawing and folksy characterization. Her portrait of *"Utrillo, Grandmère et le Chien"* struck me as deeply indigenously French.

I was disappointed in the rooms devoted to the recent masters, Picasso, Raoul Dufy, Léger, etc. They seemed unbelievably hollow and weak after the Louvre and after the Museum of the Impressionists. Matisse and Rouault showed up better here.

Joseph Floch.

RAPHAEL
SOYER

sketced
In Floch's studio

Model in Floch's studio.

Model in Floch's studio.

Chagall was well represented by his early paintings, notably his self-portrait on his wife's shoulders.

In the profusion of other paintings at the Museum I liked a few single, tortuously expressive figure pieces, one of them a self-portrait by George Gruber. Needless to say, a great deal of space was given over to the many varieties of non-representationalism —all creating the usual meaningless confusion.

The Prado

September 1964

I CAME TO THE PRADO WITH GREAT ANTICIPATION. I HAD BEEN THERE THIRTY years ago when El Greco was all the rage (due probably to the Meyer Graeffe book about him). Nevertheless at that time I preferred Velasquez, and now he loomed even greater than ever. There is something impenetrable about his painting. It is deceptively simple, aloof and warm at the same time. He painted mostly life-size, and full-length —people, horses, dogs. One gets the *feeling* of life-size.

I was really taken aback by *The Spinners*—it seemed so modern in content and spirit. I immediately thought of Courbet—he could have painted this subject. The *Las Meninas* with its interior and self-portrait also brought Courbet's *Studio* to mind. But the paintings of Velasquez are more reticent, illusive, completely non-didactic.

Of all big paintings, *Las Meninas* is the most lovable—it is faultless in composition, technique, color. The figures are universal, and timeless, in spite of their period costumes, so human in movement and gesture. The little Infanta and her two maids bloom in the darkened space of the interior. It is unfortunate to show this painting in a room by itself with the tricky mirror that reflects it stereoptically. It should be hung alongside the other work of Velasquez.

It may seem strange, but in this hall of Velasquez paintings, Degas comes to mind. Magnified to life-size, the *Repasseuses* and the *Absinthe Drinkers* would not be unlike the pictures of the great Spaniard.

I'm beginning to feel as if I've had my fill of wandering, sightseeing, even of art. I am conscience-stricken for not painting all these weeks, so much so that I've been plagued again, as I often am in such situations, by this recurring dream: Unable to remember where my studio is, I wander about in a state of amnesia, and when finally I reach my studio, I find it in semi-ruin, the door without a knob, and when, in desperation, I try to pry it open with my fingernails, it gives way, hinges and all.

154

Venice

September 1964

THE 23RD BIENNALE IN VENICE WAS WELL PUBLICIZED BY ITS SPONSORS, GOSSIPED about, debunked and derided in many circles and manicly and pontifically lauded in others. Weeks before we left for Europe, I read the massive publicity on this show of paintings and sculpture, internationally agreed upon as the art of today by the museum directors, the art critics, the art dealers, the moneyed collectors, and the speculators—the molders of our aesthetics. They have master-minded the Biennale—it's their baby.

It's impossible to describe the thousands of items in the labyrinthian array of halls and buildings. The goading of the artist by the art mart to be ever more novel has resulted in some insane productions: electrically "animated" plastic gewgaws with disgusting, maggot-like slow movements; chopped-up pianos, painstakingly but senselessly put together into meaningless and useless constructions; the now not-so-novel crushed fenders, etc. The paintings were of the usual obsessively repetitious non-objective type that we have long since become accustomed to, plus the latest variety of pop art.

There were a few genuine pieces of sculpture and paintings. Although not of great caliber, they were a relief: work by Giacommetti; a cardinal by Manzu; several pieces of sculpture by, I think, Paganin at the entrance to the Italian Pavilion; a charming portrait drawing of Picasso by a long-forgotten contemporary of his, Assas. Even a nightmarish figure by Frances Bacon seemed plausible, and next to it was an interesting small canvas, a portrait of Bacon by Lucien Freud. No wonder that the attendance was small, and from the overheard remarks, exclamations, and giggles, it seemed to us that those who did come were there out of curiosity.

One section of the Biennale served for me as an antidote to all this—the showing in the Correr Museum of the Manzu studies for the door in St. Peter's. These affirmative, living, beautifully textured and patinated bronze bas-reliefs simply negated the lifeless atmosphere generated by the rest of the Biennale.

Gabriele Mucchi.

I've been following the work of Giacomo Manzu with admiration ever since I saw his sculpture, years ago, of a child sitting on a chair. In today's artistic chaos he is among the few whose work is a testimony to the continuity of the ever-renewable tradition in art embodied in the human image.

Near the Academia a painting in the window of a gallery attracted my attention, an expressionistic, vital portrait of a woman. I went in and saw the retrospective exhibition of Gabriele Mucchi, whose work I had first noticed and liked three years ago in a Milan gallery. These paintings, drawings, and water colors were particularly interesting because although they depicted the political and social struggles in Italy during this era, they transcended mere illustrativeness by sheer paint quality and by the personality of the artist—in the tradition of Goya, Orozco, Guttuso.

I met the artist and we were able to communicate in German, of which my wife has some knowledge. We were interested to learn that this Italian had been teaching for several years in East Berlin, where he tried to break through the dogmatism of the official approach to esthetics.

Although aghast and disturbed at the contemporary art situation, Mucchi told us he was nevertheless optimistic about representationalism—that it has a great future. His manner was quiet, not emphatic. He struck me as a somewhat withdrawn intellectual, warmly appreciative of other artists.

Piazza San Marco, Venice.

From *The English Ambassadors*, by Carpaccio.

Giacomo Manzu

September 1964

WE GOT TO SEE MANZU THE LAST DAY OF OUR STAY IN ROME. A YEAR AGO I HAD a letter of introduction to him from Guttuso, but we arrived in Rome after he had already left for the country. When Guttuso gave us the letter he told us that Manzu was a quiet man, talks very little, only in Italian, "and that," said Guttuso good-humoredly and fondly, "only in dialect."

When I mentioned Manzu in our conversation with Mucchi in Venice, he spoke with warmth about the man, as well as about his art. Mucchi thought it admirable for a man like Manzu, who did the doors for St. Peter's in Rome, to have sent one hundred red roses for the funeral of the communist Togliatti.

We made a special trip to St. Peter's to see these recently installed doors. They had all the beauty and the warmth that one finds in all Manzu's work. In the lower right-hand panel was the praying figure of the late Pope John XXIII, with the inscription *Pacem in Terris*. It seemed to have a special meaning for us in this era of social and political unrest, of race riots and atomic explosions.

The visit to Manzu was arranged by a young friend of ours who drove us there in her new, noisy little car, and who also served as our interpreter. We circled around several streets near the outskirts of Rome before we finally found the Largo where Manzu's studio was—a long, low structure in a bare courtyard. We were expected, and when we rang the bell at the courtyard gate, a young woman, her face and figure like a Manzu sculpture, let us in silently and politely.

The studio was huge, uncluttered, although here and there were sculptures of all sizes, in various media. Manzu came forward—stocky, heavy-nosed, with a small mouth, warm, alert eyes. He wore a small black and white checked cloth hat, deliberately, it seemed to me, askew on his head, and a black smock—altogether a droll, sympathetic figure, a combination of laborer and comic actor.

Through the interpreter we exchanged greetings, and I tried to express to him my admiration for his work, which, I said, I have been following since I saw his

160

MANZU
ROMA
1964

RAPHAEL
SOYER

Giacomo Manzu.

Sculpture by Manzu in museum in Rome.

figure of a seated child. I told him that he seems to me to be the most painter-like of all the sculptors, that he draws on his reliefs and composes his sculptures like a painter. He seemed to understand what I was trying to convey. He said, "There's little to show in my studio." But the "little" was enough to confirm my conviction that he is one of the finest sculptors today. There was a group of small clay studies of clothed, semi-reclining female figures. Some of them were cast in bronze. On the wall above them was a life-size, very complete drawing of a model in this same pose. In one corner stood a larger than life-size plaster nude of a dancer, reaching upward on her toes, her arms high above her head. That, he told us, was a commission, to be placed in a square in Detroit. Contrasting with her was a dark carving in ebony of a mother and child, roughly hewn and unfinished, but already eloquent in its beauty.

I was impressed by the compactness and self-containment of Manzu's figures. There were no unnecessary embellishments, no protuberances, spikiness, holes, and perforations abounding in so much of the sculpture today. "Surely," I thought, "they would pass Michelangelo's test for sculpture: There is nothing superfluous that would break off if they were rolled down a hill."

But our communication was very meager because of the language barrier as well as Manzu's reticence. The frustrations of talking through an interpreter were felt by both of us. As our interpreter later commented, "Manzu doesn't talk. He just answers questions."

When I asked Manzu to pose for a sketch, he smiled and said with a twinkle in his eye: "It will be a pleasure not to work, but to watch someone else work for a change."

Although he tried to keep his head in position while responding to the interpreter, his hands kept moving, as though they were unused to being idle. They moved in sculptor's gestures.

On the way out I noticed some canvases stacked up against the wall and I asked Manzu whose they were. "They're mine," he said, "I always painted." But I saw that he didn't think enough of them to show them.

Edwin Dickinson

November 1964

AT LAST I PAINTED EDWIN DICKINSON, HAVING BEEN AFTER HIM FOR ALMOST A YEAR. After many disappointments and postponements, I brought my paint box and canvas to his studio and painted him there. When I knocked on his door, the slight, bearded Dickinson appeared with the suddenness of a Jack-in-the-Box, a tasseled red Turkish fez on his head. With a roguish look, his arms akimbo, he said, "How would you like to paint me like this?"

Very soon, however, we settled down to work. He posed seriously. Every half hour by his watch, he would take a rest, during which he circled his small studio several times. Now and then he would pick up a fragment of a canvas mounted crudely on pressed wood, and show it to me. About one he commented: "Some eyes that girl had!" It really was just a picture of one eye, no other feature of the face, on a flesh-painted canvas, a beautifully rendered blue eye. Another small unfinished painting was of a girl's head, with very black hair: "Some gal she was," and he clicked his tongue admiringly, "a very beautiful head of hair!" These canvases were very dry and seemed to have been painted a long time ago.

Dickinson posed very quietly. Once in a while he would say to himself, or to me: "I enjoy being with my brethren" (meaning the artists). The chair he sat on was wide and low, and I had to sit down, too, to see him more or less at eye level, which made me uncomfortable because I usually stand when I do these studies. I could not judge the proportions too well, and soon it seemed to me that I was making his head bigger than life and I was unhappy about it. Dickinson is really a slight man with a delicate face. As I worked on the portrait, however, it seemed to lose its over-size quality and I felt more satisfied with it. Dickinson never looked at what I was doing even though we sat so near one another. As he took his walks around the room he sensitively avoided looking at the canvas, not to embarrass his "brother artist" in the initial stages of his work. I was inwardly grateful for that. "Of course," he said,

Detail from a life study of Edwin Dickinson.

"I am very much interested in what you're doing, and I'll come to see your big picture."

I have often noticed how unpretentious and modest, even austere, are the studios of some of America's best-known artists—Hopper, Levine, Dickinson—quite different from the well-appointed studios of their European counterparts. Dickinson's was bare, neat and orderly. There was little furniture there, only one easel. The whitewashed walls were decorated with pale maps of the Mediterranean and of the Greek Isles. Two old violins were hanging on the wall, horizontally, one above the other. One was unusually red in color—"the reddest violin I have ever seen," said Dickinson. "I will pick it up one of these days and start sawing again," he said, pointing to them.

He held up a maul-stick and called my attention to its grace, the texture of the old wood, and to the rubber tip which he himself neatly attached to keep it from slipping on the surface of the canvas. On the wall there was also a double parallel ruler used in navigation. He showed me how to work it: he put it down flat on the map which was on the wall, moved each ruler alternately, saying, "You waltz it up to the compass rose." Although I understood but little of this, there was something very likeable about the way he said it.

Dickinson put his hand in his pocket, took something out of it, and let it fall to the floor. It was a plastic clothespin. "Did you hear the click?" he asked me. "As I was coming here a woman threw it out the window, and it fell with a click at my feet. When she shut the window I quickly picked it up and put it in my pocket. It's nice, so white."

On the floor, leaning against the wall, were old casts of the fragmentary Elgin Marbles, horses' heads and riders, revealing his well-known love for Greece, so often expressed in his paintings. Somehow the austerity of Greece was felt in this American artist's studio. Suddenly he said to me during one of his rests: "I can sing a Greek song for you," and he sang one of the monotonous Greek folk songs.

In a pleasant resonant voice he speaks in complex, rambling sentences that often end with prepositions. He gave me the impression in his conversation during the sittings that he was obliged to assume family responsibilities as well as teaching responsibilities. And his time for painting is precious. It takes him so long to finish a painting, sometimes years. "And anyhow," he said, "my paintings are never completed. My 'finished' paintings are only three-fifths finished." I liked his arithmetical exactness—it is so much like him, meticulous and neat, like the lecture he was going to deliver soon at some university on "Application of the Principles of the Housekeeping of the Palette."

As the time of the first sitting was coming to a close, he said, "Don't forget to remind me to show you that book," and he turned his eyes toward a pile of small old books on the table. It turned out to be an old, worn little book, with a few illustrations, about some chateau in France where da Vinci was said to have died. He called my attention to a reproduction of a very ornate and complex staircase, which was supposed to have been designed by da Vinci. His interest in this was meaningful to me, having often seen in Dickinson's paintings architectural forms or staircases.

I finished the study, a head and shoulders on a large canvas (which I embellished with a sketch of a Greek horse). I put the canvas down, which Dickinson had not yet looked at, face against the wall. Then he pulled out a few old studies in oil, gray and brown in tone, which he painted as a student, with William M. Chase, of whom he spoke with respect and admiration. And finally a larger canvas, not of his student days, depicting a street, with a painting of the same street in the foreground. The effect was double-imaged, surrealistic. He painted this many years ago. Dickinson considered this also not completed—"I will get to it again someday, if I'm spared."

December 1964

NOW THAT I HAVE FINALLY MADE THE STUDY OF EDWIN DICKINSON, AND THE DRAW-
ings of my daughter Mary for the figure of the girl holding the tray, I am beginning
to work steadily again on the big painting. The composition is rounded out, all the
figures are now painted in. I have been working on the Eakins paintings that serve as
a background from the colored reproductions in Fairfield Porter's book on Thomas
Eakins. (As I am working on this huge canvas with the same small brushes I generally
use, numbers 2, 3, 4, 5, I amusingly recall how I watched Rivera in the early thirties,
painting his large complex, many-figured murals with a tiny brush.)

I went to the Brooklyn Museum to look at the Eakins painting of the sculptor
William Rush, and I was amazed how untruthful is the reproduction of it in the
Fairfield Porter book. The original is predominantly brown, without any of the
delicate shades of green, lavender and pink found in the reproduction. Next day I
repainted that picture in the background.

Sketch
of Mary serving drinks
for Homage To
Eakins

RAPHAEL SOYER
1965

Mary serving drinks. Study for *Homage to Thomas Eakins*.

Charles Daniel

December 1964

THE TELEPHONE RANG. A SHARP VOICE, CRACKED WITH AGE, WAS ON THE OTHER END of the line. "Did you get my note? I sent you a clipping from the newspaper, a review of Hopper's show . . . I don't understand any more what's going on in art . . . The One who created people gave them very low intelligence . . . Look at the T.V. programs they enjoy . . . We've had ten thousand years of culture and most people will never know any better."

This was the voice of Charles Daniel. He is now eighty-six years old: "Soon I'll be eighty-seven years old, and I'm getting frightened," he said recently. Though once tall and broad-shouldered, he is now frail and toothless. His mind is very clear. I often get notes, clippings, art magazines or copies of American Heritage from him, with fond inscriptions to me and my wife.

In 1928 I took a painting I had just finished to the Daniel Gallery. This was done at the suggestion of Guy Pène du Bois with whom I had studied, and who saw the painting. The gallery was situated on the top floor of a small, charming red-brick building at 600 Madison Avenue, since demolished, of course. A tall ruddy-faced man, Charles Daniel, looked at the painting, showed it to his cadaverous associate, a green-looking, shaking individual, who, I later learned, was Clarence Hartpence, a frustrated poet. There was a murmured consultation between the two, then Mr. Daniel came back to me and said, "Leave this painting here. When you have twelve such pictures, we will give you a one man exhibition."

It was as simple as that in those days, at least for me. There were only about a dozen galleries then and the Daniel Gallery was known for its high priesthood in art. It was there that the best contemporary work produced in this country was exhibited. Besides, it had an aim—to discover and promote young painters who showed some individuality in their work. When I came to the Daniel Gallery it already had on its roster, among others, Kuniyoshi, Alex Brook, Peter Blume, Preston Dickinson, Nicolai Cikovsky, Karl Knaths. In 1929 I had my twelve paintings, and they were

170

Charles Daniel.

exhibited at the Daniel Gallery. Henry McBride, the avant-garde critic of that period known for his sophisticated understanding of art and his engaging style, favorably reviewed the exhibition, and then and there I embarked upon my career of painting. But 1929 was a fateful year, and in the beginning of the depression that followed, this gallery was forced out of existence. It never was able to make a comeback.

By now I no longer count the passing years. But a long time after his gallery closed, Charles Daniel was the guest of honor at a dinner party given by its former members. Yasuo Kuniyoshi was still alive then and was the charming m.c. at that party. We all made drawings that were presented to him in a portfolio that night. Everyone made a speech, and I still remember that I said, "When I was young my teacher, Guy Pène du Bois looked at a painting of mine and sent me to the Daniel Gallery with it. Now I am a teacher, and every once in a while I become interested in a talented student, and I regret that there is no Daniel Gallery today to which I can send him."

Since then I have been seeing Charles Daniel at intervals. Suddenly I would get a call that he's in town and is coming up. He is full of stories of the art world way back in the early 1900's. He mentions long-forgotten names of painters, collectors, museum directors, and critics. In his New Yorkese English this former gallery director, who gave up saloon-keeping for art-dealing, talks about how difficult it was in those days to sell the new art, not yet accepted in this country. He remembers how the rich homes of the collectors in Back Bay Boston or on Fifth Avenue were filled with paintings by John Murphy, Dodge McKnight, and others, and how hard it was to educate them to appreciate John Marin, Charles Demuth, Preston Dickinson.

Charles Daniel is puzzled and completely bewildered by the paintings of today. What he sees on Madison Avenue and on 57th Street violates the meaning of art for him and is beyond his comprehension. But art is still the only interest of this amazing old man.

Self-portraits. Studies from life.

Reginald Marsh

February 1965

FOR THE FIGURE OF REGINALD MARSH IN THE EAKINS PAINTING, I AM COPYING AN old portrait I did of him in 1941, which the Detroit Museum let me have for this purpose. At first I had sketched his head in from a black-and-white reproduction of that portrait. As I am working on Reggie now (the only one of this group who is no longer alive—he died in 1954), many memories come to me of our relationship when we were neighbors in a building overlooking Union Square Park. I am including in these informal pages an article I wrote at the time of Reggie's death for *Reality, A Journal of Artists' Opinion:*

Now that Reginald Marsh is gone we may expect the usual appraisal and re-appraisal of his accomplishments. His thousands of drawings, prints, and paintings will be categorized and catalogued and he will finally be pigeonholed in his proper place in American art. My task is not in this field of appraisal. Having known him for many years, I would like rather to impart my memories and impressions of him. Actually there is nothing startling or dramatic for me to tell. One constant memory of him is that of a man always at work, drawing, painting, experimenting with different techniques, but above all drawing, drawing, drawing.

I remember painting a portrait of him. After half an hour of posing he could not bear being inactive and so he took a small copper plate, concealed it in his hand and, while holding the pose, managed to make an etching of me at the same time.

He had an intense and consuming interest in art. I would find him in various museums in New York, Washington, Philadelphia, studying one painting or another, often through a magnifying glass, oblivious to everything else around him. He must have passed this absorbing interest on to his students, for once I saw him with a group of them in the museum. He was not lecturing, not telling anything in words, but again looking intently at paintings, and his students, a silent and enthralled group, as absorbed as their teacher, almost looking like Marsh, their faces as close to the paintings as his was. Occasionally I meet some of Marsh's former students and I am always impressed by their enduring memory of him as an inspiring teacher.

Long ago in the 1930's, once after a day's work in the middle of the week, a party happened spontaneously in my studio, for we were young enough then to be spontaneous about such things. A few artists were there, a sculptor from across the street who has since been killed in one of the wars; a vivacious young girl who used to pose for the artists in the building; and a Union Square character, a homeless man who attached himself to the artists, posed, ran errands for them and tidied their studios. We called him The Orphan. In the course of time the people became a little high and the first to pass out was The Orphan. Immediately Reginald Marsh, who had all along been drinking silently and broodingly, went into action. With unexpected tenderness he guided The Orphan to the cot, laid him gently down, removed his shoes and covered him. Like a dream, I remember the dry skin through the holes in the socks and the expression of concern on Reggie's face.

There was something childlike about Reggie. He took unabashed delight in little things: the staircase in the interior of the studio leading up to the roof; the Senator's chauffeured car, at his disposal in Washington. Like a small boy he had a great love for locomotives and tugboats, spending much time on the waterfront and near railroad tracks, drawing and painting them. This trait added to his mature knowledge and understanding, gave him a special charm, and endeared him to his friends.

I visited his home recently. There, on the walls beside Marsh's paintings, were a portrait by Eakins, a youthful portrait of Marsh in pastels by Peggy Bacon, a satirical tinted drawing by Guy Pène du Bois, and paintings and drawings by Kuniyoshi, Kathrine Schmidt, Felicia Meyers (Reggie's wife). I asked Mrs. Marsh if there was anything in the form of an autobiography left by Reggie, for as yet no monograph exists about Reggie's work. It is amazing how little is printed and published about our own artists during their lifetime in our country, rich as it is. After rummaging around, Mrs. Marsh found some articles about him and his work by his fellow artists Benton, Laning, Curry and others.

But I was most impressed by a comment that was written by Marsh himself in an old catalogue of one of his shows: "Painting is new to me, but I will conquer it."

February 1965

WELL, IT SEEMS I STARTED SOMETHING WITH MY HOMAGE TO EAKINS. THESE DAYS it's such an off-beat thing to do—a huge representational painting, a group portrait of men. The news that I was doing this reached the ears of the avid collector, Joseph H. Hirshhorn. My dealer brought him, together with his curator, Abram Lerner, to my studio, and a collector's scoop was made by his quick purchase of the entire work—the as yet unfinished large painting, plus all the studies for it. This event was reported in the art page of the Sunday *Times,* with a reproduction of the painting and a photograph of myself in front of it.

Hirshhorn's inclusion of this work in his famous collection pleased me very much. I sent him the following letter next day:

Dear Joe,

I am so pleased that you have acquired my paintings of the *Homage to Eakins* project. Secretly I had hoped all along that you would do so because more than anything I wanted these canvases to be part of a great collection.

It was quite an undertaking. There were moments when I didn't feel equal to the task. I would ask myself: what prompted me to do a composition of such magnitude and of such content? It seemed, on the surface, such an untimely thing to do. But then some of the greatest painters worked against their own *Zeitgeist*.

I have been wanting to do this for a long time—a group portrait of life-size figures. My admiration for Eakins provided the setting for such a composition. And since I know that you, too, are a great admirer of Eakins, it gives me heart to bring to completion this group of paintings. Thank you.

This seems to be the end of the book. The painting, however, is not yet finished. I am working on it now, inch by inch, and am beginning to have the usual anxieties about overworking it. So, this chronicle ends with an expression of anxiety. Characteristic of artists—ever apprehensive, anxious, and uncertain.

176

Index

177